TALES OF ANGELIC UPSTARTS

BOOK ONE

THE CXNTERBURY TALES

MICK N BAKER

Tales of Angelic Upstarts					The Cxnterbury Tales

Copyright © 2021 Michael Baker

The moral right of the author has been asserted.

All characters and events in this publication are based on real people, lives and events… And some aren't.

All rights reserved

No part of this publication may be reproduced, stored in a retrieval system, or transmitted in any form or by any means, without the prior permission in writing of the author, nor be otherwise circulated in any form of binding or cover other than that in which it is published and without a similar condition including this condition being imposed on the subsequent purchaser.

Tales of Angelic Upstarts					The Cxnterbury Tales

To Chris, Jess and Abbie

For Mum and Dad
With life comes understanding

The Cxnterbury Tales - Book One
Tales of an Angelic Upstart

Chapter 1   -   Sod's Law
Chapter 2   -   Into the Ruts
Chapter 3   -   The Glorious Bar E
Chapter 4   -   C.J. Gets His Just (Sunshine) Desserts
Chapter 5   -   The Frog and Breeze Block
Chapter 6   -   Where am I? You are in The Village
Chapter 7   -   The Thief, The Voyeur and The Brother
Chapter 8   -   Don't Bullshit, A Bullshitter
Chapter 9   -   Teardrop
Chapter 10 -   Rock Against Racism
Chapter 11 -   A Dedicated Follower of Fashion
Chapter 12 -   Judy is a What?
Chapter 13 -   Cold Christmas
Chapter 14 -   Ain't No Feeble Bastard
Chapter 15 -   Mr. January in Beastiality Monthly
Chapter 16 -   Nigel Osbourne Gets Launched
Chapter 17 -   End Product

"He who repeats a tale after a man,

Is bound to say, as nearly as he can,

Each single word, if he remembers it

However rudely spoken or unfit,

Or else the tale he tells will be untrue,

The things invented and the phrases new."

- Geoffrey Chaucer

Tales of Angelic Upstarts   The Cxnterbury Tales

Chapter 1

Sod's Law

Richard Hale School was founded in 1617 by rich merchant Richard Hale, who wished to 'erect a grammar school for the instruction of children in the Latin tongue and other literature in the town of Hertford.' In 1977, after over three centuries of educational excellence, to give everyone the opportunity of a grammar school education, they decided to let the comprehensive kids in, which was bad timing for them, as not only did they let in kids with lower abilities, like myself, they let in the most energetic, fiercest youth movement ever to hit these shores. Punk Rock.

I was mostly well-behaved in the first and second years, come the third year though, I realised that my future lay outside the confinement of classes and the restrictive nature of education, so I sought out other kids who were into what I was into; I soon found a kid called Iain Lancer.

Iain and me spent all of our time talking about Punk Rock, girls, how much we hated the teachers, and sometimes, if we were really bored, we would even talk about schoolwork, but that didn't happen too often. I liked Iain, he was always up for a laugh, we brought plenty of chaos to the classes that we shared together.

In the run-up to the end of the third year though, with exams that would lead to us being streamed, Iain began to knuckle down, hit the books, worse still he was showing an interest in The Jam, a band who after flirting with the punk scene at its conception and getting their breakthrough, as a result, had finally come out as Mods. I thought it was time to find some other mates; kids who were still kicking back against the system, kids who didn't think The Jam's

'Setting Sons' album was iconic, on the same level as 'Never Mind the Bollocks' by the Sex Pistols.

One day, Iain and me were sitting in our form room talking, when he mentioned that there was a kid in our year called Richard Townsend who loved punk, he told me that I would recognise him easily by his hair. Sure enough, as I walked down the corridor on my way to the dinner hall at lunchtime that day, I saw Richard standing in the dinner queue, he had this wild blonde spiked up hair, like Billy Idol, the vocalist with Generation X. I thought he looked cool, so strolled up to him.

I gave him a nod, "I like your hair, mate."

"Cheers," he said, laughing nervously.

"Are you into Punk, then?" I asked.

He nodded back at this random stranger with his short ginger brown spiked hair, who had just randomly struck up a conversation with him, like it was obvious. I asked him what bands he was into, he replied in a broad Mancunian accent that he liked The Ruts, the UK Subs, who I also liked, he also said his favourite band by far was Generation X.

I smiled, "Yeah, I could have guessed that."

Richard laughed, saw I was just being friendly and offered me a cut into the dinner queue, which was handy as it was about a mile long. A couple of kids standing behind got miffed, so we told them to piss off, made our way into the dinner hall together, sat down, ate some of the brown gruel-like paste they were serving as food and spent the rest of break talking about punk rock.

Tales of Angelic Upstarts			The Cxnterbury Tales

Richard and me got on straight away, not only did we like the same music, we found, we both shared the same warped sense of humour, so we started hanging out together, either in our shared classes where we created mayhem or out in the playground playing the traditional Richard Hale game; Chuckers.

Chuckers was played by up to a playground full of kids, someone chucked a tennis ball against a wall, and anyone who was in front of the person who caught the ball would get the ball chucked at them as hard as the catcher could throw it. Not only was it a good laugh; it was the perfect way to pay back the many swots we had at Richard Hale for their hideous classroom toadyism. In most cases when the ball was caught, the catcher would identify one of these swots and sting them up, sometimes the hapless swot wasn't even playing, he still got his legs stung up; most of the time, it was more to do with who was in range, than who was actually playing.

Richard started coming to my house too, where we would go up into my bedroom, play my small collection of 7-inch singles on my cheap white plastic record player. On one occasion, a mate of mine said that the sound was so bad on it that he could see puke coming out of the speakers, I didn't care, it sounded fine to me. On one such visit, Richard noticed my split wood Hondo guitar propped up against the wall, keys out, and asked me if I could play. I smiled, hoping he was going to ask, and told him that even though I hadn't been playing long, I knew a few chords and I had written some brilliant tracks. I asked if he wanted to hear some of them.

I had picked it up even before he had time to say 'Yeah, go on then, Skinner' and began playing. Richard smiled nodding along, looking impressed, so after I had played him a couple of brilliant tracks and showed him some equally brilliant lyrics, I asked if he would like to sing on them, and although he didn't want to be a singer, he said he'd give it a go, and we started practising.

A couple of weeks later, we were The Sods, had around ten tracks including 'Kids on the Street', 'Like it at Home', 'Bleak Outlook', 'Stupid Rules' and 'Nice Girls', which I thought was our best track by far. I was particularly pleased with the way the chorus came across, when Richard sang 'Oh how I wish I could get one of those niiiice girrrrrls.' I would play E, G and D chords whilst chanting 'oh, oh, oh, oh' as the harmony. Sometimes when we played it, I would get goosebumps on my arms and down the back of my neck, it was that good.

I wasn't the only one, Richard loved it too, so we decided to use it as our opening track on The Sod's first album, named 'The Sods live at the Lyceum', which we recorded in my bedroom using my mum's tape recorder. To make it sound authentic, we used the cheering and audience hubbub from the 'Live at the Roxy' album. It was a simple process; we would play our track then as it came to its end, I would cue up The Roxy album's audience cheering and clapping on my plastic record player, we would say, 'cheers', 'cheers… Nice one, thank you', 'cheers… This is our next track' and when we got near to the end of the tape on side one of our debut album 'The Sods live at the Lyceum' Richard said, 'OK cheers… We're going off for a cup of tea now, see you in a minute' and the Roxy audience roared back its approval. It took us a whole hour to complete the album and as we sat back in our makeshift dressing room, on my bed in my bedroom, we listened in wonder at how good we sounded.

In fact, we were so pleased with it, that we made a special trip to a passport booth on the way back from school the next day, had some band photos taken, black and white of course, to give it that extra street punk feel. Once I got home, I cut them out, glued them onto some coloured card with our logo above to complete the album cover. I found the entire process of writing, playing and recording music, exhilarating, and spent hours at it, so much so that on some nights my mum would bang on my bedroom wall, telling me, 'Stop and get to bed! You have school in the morning'. It was after our next album, 'The Sods Live at the Electric Ballroom', which we recorded in my garage for better acoustics, using the audience recording from my mum's Rolling Stone's album 'Get Yer Ya-Ya's out', that I began to think it was all a bit make believe, immature, what we were doing had run its course. I believed The Sods needed to move forward now, or we would end up like Spizz Oil, another punk duo without a bass player or a drummer, who I thought would have been so much better with a rhythm section.

One evening after a particularly good practice where we introduced another track, 'Ain't got nothing to do' to our already burgeoning repertoire, Richard and me sat down with steaming cups of tea and had a band meeting, deciding unanimously, that it was time to find ourselves a rhythm section, starting with a bass player, then once we had a bass player, hopefully, they would know someone who was into punk and played the drums.

Paul 'Rat' Collins was into punk, played bass, and even though I didn't know him well and hardly spoke to him because he seemed to be up himself like he was a bit *punkier than thou*, I strutted up to him confidently during first break one day, inviting him round mine to audition for my band. Rat seemed a bit taken aback at my opening confidence, gaping at me as I told him what we needed to take the band forward, the more I spoke, the more enthusiastic he got. Once I was done, Rat smiled broadly, telling me that although he was a bit rusty, having not played in a band for a long time, he was well up for it and asked when I wanted to do it.

"Oh, don't worry, it's fine you'll pick it up," I replied, charitably, arranging his audition at my house for the coming Saturday.

On the Saturday morning, I heard my doorbell ring. Answering it, I found a scruffy, bald-headed old bloke standing on my doorstep with an amp balanced on his shoulder. Behind him stood a grinning Rat, with another one on his.

"Hi, Baker," said Rat from over Baldy's other shoulder.

"Hi, you alright Rat?"

A visibly straining Baldy pushed past me, "Where do you want them, then?" he asked, impatiently.

I smiled uncertainly, pointing them in the direction of my bedroom and stood back, nervously watching, as they tentatively navigated their way up our wooden stairs, hoping that they didn't bounce them off the walls or worse still, drop them completely.

In the meantime, my old man had come out of the lounge to see what all the commotion was, he sighed deeply, placed his hands on his hips, standing, boggle-eyed, watching all of this heavy electronic equipment going up his stairs in disbelief, waiting for the inevitable.

My old man stared at me accusingly, "What's going on, Michael?"

"Er, we are just auditioning a bass player, Dad."

"Oh, are you now?"

A loud thump shook the floor of my bedroom, the old man took a sharp intake of breath, I held mine, another thump, then Rat and Baldy marched back downstairs, Baldy wiping at his feverish brow.

"Is that it, Rat?" I asked, hopefully.

Rat shook his head, "No," he said, distractedly. He and Baldly pounded back outside, collected another couple of bass bins, entered the hallway, haltingly shouldering them upstairs as well.

"OK, right, that's it… We are going out!" Said my old man, tersely. His peaceful Saturday morning, lying in tatters.

Once all of Rat's gear was in my room, I stood by the window and watched, waiting until mum and the old man had gone out, which didn't take very long. The Sods' audition began. Rat powered up his rig, picked up his bass guitar and launched into 'Theme', the opening track on P.I.L's first edition album, making the floor shake under our feet. Richard and me sat back and marvelled as he played the whole of the first P.I.L. album, note for note, I doubted even Jah Wobble himself would have been able to play this well live- we were absolutely stunned, the guy was brilliant and then, as he played the last notes of 'Fodderstompf', it was our turn.

I wasn't sure if I wanted to play him our tracks, or even play in front of him after seeing how good he was, he was in a totally different league to us. I glanced over at Richard, whose face sat somewhere between a look of deep respect and high trepidation. Rat grinned lopsidedly at us both, smoothly unplugged his bass, gave me a friendly nod and sat down on my bed expectantly, so I picked up my guitar and began strumming away. It felt wrong. All of my confidence disappeared and then with a dawning realisation, I saw that the tracks I had written were shit, in fact they were worse than shit, they were childlike, embarrassing, and as the track ground to its weary end, I peeked over at Rat and I could tell he was thinking the exact same thing.

Rat smiled pleasantly, "I tell you what. If we both go through my amp together, we might be able to do something with what you played there."

I told him uncomfortably that I didn't have a jack plug, and he gave me a look of pure pity and shook his head. That was it, the audition was over; we had failed badly.

Rat and Baldy, his follicly challenged Passepartout, left later that afternoon, leaving Richard and me to ponder our future as musicians. We soon agreed that The Sods should be disbanded with immediate effect and to show there would be no going back we tossed all of our live albums into the dustbin. I wanted to burn them on my mum's flowerbed in the back garden as a gesture of our future intent, but I felt she and my old man had suffered enough for one day.

Once Richard had left, I vowed to put my 'lyric' writing aside and concentrate on getting my guitar playing up to a decent standard, so I would never have to go through that same kind of embarrassment again; I also vowed to buy a couple of jack leads too. I doubted Rat would say anything to anyone at school, he was a pretty cool kid, I was still dreading going back on Monday though, and the piss-taking I could be faced with. I mean, fucking hell, what kind of guitar player doesn't have any jack leads? A shit one!!!

I bought a chord book, with six jack leads from Ware Music, the next time it was open and began practising in earnest. If Richard was around, I would show him a few chords, he took to it really quickly and started looking into buying a guitar for himself. If we were going to be in a band together, it was a bass player we needed, so Richard suggested that he should get a bass guitar and be our bass player. Yeah, of course that makes a lot more sense, I thought, it would be great to be in a band, but it would be even better to be in a band with your mates. It was decided then, Richard would learn how to play the bass guitar and once he was up to a decent standard himself, we would start looking for a drummer and a singer.

A few weeks later, Richard went out with his jazz loving old man, to buy his bass guitar, and unsurprisingly he came back with a jazz bass, which I should have seen coming. I was hoping he would get one like Sid Vicious; the classic white with the black scratch plates, with the four tuning keys on the top. Richard's one, however, was blue and red with an all-over pearly effect, if that wasn't bad enough, the keys were two up and two down. I thought it looked sad, like something the Bee Gee's might play in their sequinned suits; it was well poncy. I didn't say anything though and later when he plugged it into my newly acquired amp, turned the bass levels right up, it sounded fine, in fact it rumbled my floorboards just like Rat's one.

Chapter Two

Into The Ruts

It was around this time I went to my first gig, The Ruts, at the Moonlight Club in West Hampstead. Richard and me loved The Ruts, and when we read about their up-and-coming gig in the music paper Sounds, we checked out where the venue was, the location of the nearest tube station and the times of the trains, which is where we saw we might have a problem. If we left the gig at eleven when it was due to end, we would only have half an hour to get from West Hampstead to Tottenham Hale on the tube, to catch the last train home. Richard found out that from London Underground, the specified journey time was thirty minutes. It would be cutting it fine, to say the least. I told him not to worry about it but unfortunately, he did, he told his old man of his worries and he in turn told Richard that in light of what he had told him he couldn't go. Richard was devastated, so was I, however, I had already got the green light from my parents and had told them that I would be sleeping over at Richard's after the gig, so they wouldn't know where I was, or what I was doing, so there was no way I wasn't going.

On the day of the gig, I caught an early train up to London arriving at the Moonlight Club at around five o'clock, only to find the place was totally deserted, so I sat on the steps that led up to the venue's entrance, watching London go by. It was bustling, full of life, I immersed myself in it, revelling in its vibrancy. A while later, a tall black guy strolled up to me, gave me a friendly nod, picked out a step for himself and sat down, introducing himself as Mannah. It turned out Mannah worked as a roadie for the Ruts. I sat back listening in amazement as he told me all about what it was like being their roadie and some of the things that they got up to while they were on the road, he also told me some stories about Malcolm

Owen, which he said I shouldn't pass on, especially to the music newspapers Sounds and the New Musical Express.

I couldn't believe what I was hearing, or who I was hearing it from either, it was hard to digest, then it got even better for me, when I saw Malcolm Owen, Paul Fox, Segs and Dave Ruffy nonchalantly strolling down the street towards us. Malcolm Owen waved at Mannah, the four of them joining us on the steps, where Paul Fox pulled out a packet of cigarettes, handing them around, offering me one too, which I gratefully accepted. Mannah had told me that The Ruts were good people and easy to talk to. I soon found he was right, they put me at ease and my initial nerves dissipated. Dave Ruffy thought it was hilarious that I had got to the gig so early, telling me I must either be a proper Ruts fan or didn't understand how long it took to get from my house into London. I told him it was probably a bit of both, which sent him into fits of laughter. Malcolm Owen made a long roll up and after smoking some, he handed it to Mannah, who smoked a bit more of it and handed it onto me.

"Oh no, maybe not," said Mannah, handing it to Dave Ruffy

I didn't know what it was or what they were doing, it was strange them all having to smoke the same cigarette. Once they all had smoked some of it, Malcolm Owen, flicked the butt away, stretched his arms crucifix like and said, "OK we'd better get moving, it's time."

Malcolm, Dave, Segs and Paul stood up, shook my hand, thanked me for coming, hoped that I would enjoy the show and with one final wave they disappeared with Mannah around the back of the Moonlight Club, leaving me to my own thoughts again. I let out a deep breath and leant back on my step, still trying to digest it all. I

thought, Bloody hell… I've just met the Ruts… I have just met The Ruts and not only that, they were really friendly, approachable and interested in what I had to say… I can't wait to tell Richard. I wished he would have been here to see it too.
A while later, The Moonlight Club doors opened, I rushed in and went straight to the bar where I spent the last of my meagre change on a pint of lager. I took my precious pint to a spot right in the front of the stage, dead centre, and waited in anticipation, sipping slowly from my drink to make it last. It was still early, and soon I was busting for a piss, I wasn't going anywhere though, as the place was filling up quickly, there was no way I was going to lose my prime spot. I shuffled from foot to foot for a while, watching the place fill up. Punks with their spiked-up hair, ripped t-shirts and bondage trousers, crowded in around me, I soon forgot all about my full bladder, and once again, I wished that my mate Richard was here with me to see it all.

In a mass of excitement and expectation, the Ruts came on around nine o'clock. Malcolm Owen grinned at us, knowing what was coming, and they launched straight into 'Savage Circle'. I had listened to their early sessions on the John Peel show, I had bought their first single on people unit records, I had all their singles on Virgin Records, I had bought their first album 'The Crack' on its release day and now, here they were standing just a few feet away from me, live, loud, right in my face. I was totally blown away by the energy that they were throwing out, they played all of the tracks I had listened to a hundred times: 'Babylon's Burning', 'In A Rut', 'Dope for Guns', 'H-Eyes', 'Sus', 'It Was Cold' and of course their opener, my favourite 'Savage Circle', which took the roof off the small club. I was down at the front the whole night, rammed up against the stage, totally in awe of them, shouting out the chorus' back to them, pogoing, sweating, pushing, being pushed and loving every second of it.

The Ruts finished their set, the first encore began and I briefly thought about trains, not for long though, because I wasn't going anywhere, I was living in the moment, what happened after that moment meant nothing to me, nothing at all.

I left the gig feeling on top of the world, it wasn't only me who felt that way, all the punks who streamed out of the Moonlight Club on that cold night felt the same, and with that feeling came a great sense of unity, camaraderie, like it was our time now.

It turned out Richard's old man's concerns were well-founded, I did miss the last train home and to be honest I really didn't care, it was just another part of the adventure. I stretched out on a wooden bench at Tottenham Hale station, replaying the gig over in my mind, the images coming back thick and fast. As the first chill of the night air touched me, I thought of The Ruts track 'It was Cold', particularly the end where the track fades into the sound of an icy wind blowing, I pulled my military jacket closer to me. 'It was cold, it was night', it fucking was too, too cold to be lying on a bench, so I got up, jumped up and down to get the blood moving again, and once it was, I thought let's go, have a look about.

I walked out of the station onto the empty streets of Tottenham through empty car parks, quiet shopping malls and then as the sky lightened in the east, totally knackered, I found shelter under some trees in a park and crashed out, drifting off into a cold, fitful sleep.

*

I shuddered awake, daybreak, the sun gently probing the milky, early morning sky in the east, the moon retreating in the west, I stretched my arms wide, shivering to my core, trying to rid myself of the cold chill of the night that had got right inside my bones.

A chill slithered down my spine, I went to tuck my jacket inside my trousers, and saw there was a small brown dog sniffing at my leg, its owner standing well back, mouth wide open, gawking, like he thought I was dead. I smiled back at him and waved feebly.

"It's OK mate, I'm fine," I said, gently pushing the dog away with my knee.

A small dog it might have been, but I didn't trust it anywhere near my bollocks, they had almost been frozen off already, I thought one little nip, and they might detach altogether.

"Hmm… OK, well, if, you're sure?" The dog owner said, doubtfully, scrutinising the scruff spread out on the grass, shaking like a leaf.

"I'm fine mate, cold that's all," I explained.

"Toby, leave it… Come on, boy," The dog owner said.

Toby gave me a couple more sniffs just in case he missed something the first time around, then satisfied that he hadn't, he trotted off in search of something more interesting to smell. His owner following closely behind, with a bag of freshly laid shit swinging to and fro in his hand.

Once my potential rescuers had disappeared, I continued tucking my jacket into my trousers and stood up stiffly, still feeling the bite of the cold in my muscles. Then, as the circulation in my legs returned, I padded back up to Tottenham Hale station, where I got the first train of the day back to Ware.

In bronze sunshine, I alighted at Ware station, I just had to tell Richard, so instead of going home I went straight up to his place and knocked the door. A sleepy looking Pam, Richard's step mum answered it, seeing the state of me, she invited me in and disappeared into the kitchen, to fetch some food for the poor starving kid.

Pam re-emerged shortly afterwards with a cup of steaming hot tea and about half a loaf's worth of toast with butter and jam, telling me to help myself. I thanked her, I was ravenous and dived straight in, soon, Richard and his old man came downstairs, joining me to have their breakfast. I told them about how brilliant The Ruts had been live, through mouthfuls of toast, how I had met them outside before the gig, through a pint of tea, and of course all about the travel difficulties, which they thought were hilarious. A few hours later, my belly full, feeling warm again, I said I had better go, as my mum and dad would be wondering where I was, so I thanked Pam and head for the front door.

On his doorstep, Richard told me that his old man didn't believe that I had spent the night sleeping in a park in Tottenham, as he couldn't believe anyone would be that stupid, which had us both cracking up laughing.

*

A few days later when we were back at school, Richard swore to me that he would never miss another gig, so for the next couple of weeks, he harangued his old man incessantly, mercilessly, unwaveringly, promising him that he would be careful not to miss the last train home, then finally, reluctantly and with a great foreboding his old man eventually agreed. Now Richard had got the green light from his old man, there was no stopping us. Over the next few months, we went to see a lot of punk bands play in London, UK Subs at the Lyceum was our first gig together, it was a night to remember too; despite the security guards' best efforts, most of the audience ended up on stage with the band.

Once again, I saw the same kind of punk camaraderie I had witnessed at The Ruts gig, when a couple of kids with Mohicans, helped Richard and me up onto the stage, where we spent the rest of the night lying directly underneath the Sub's guitarist Nicky Garret as he powered through their 'Brand New Age' set.

The Ruts soon followed, who were a lot more popular than when I had seen them at the cramped Moonlight Club, they headlined at the Electric Ballroom in Camden. Richard and me saw The Damned at Rainbow, The Lurkers at Dingwall's, Stiff little Fingers at the Marque, all of their support acts, we also saw a strange line-up of a pre-Malcolm McLaren, Adam and the Ants supported by skinhead band the Angelic Upstarts, which worked out surprisingly well, eventually of course we saw Richard's favourites Generation X at the Forum, who were a lot heavier live than I thought they would be, and I enjoyed them nearly as much as he did. If there was a punk band playing in London that we liked, we'd do all we could to get there and most of the time, one way or another we got there; it was like our raison d'être - we go to gigs, therefore we are.

Chapter 3

The Glorious Bar E

If we weren't going to gigs or hanging out, Richard and me would both be practising hard on our respective instruments. Richard was picking the bass up quickly. Within a couple of weeks, he could play the first three Generation X's singles, the B-sides, most of Valley of the Dolls and was about halfway through 'The Crack' by The Ruts. It was totally different for me; I was struggling and had come to a dead end on my Hondo. I knew what I wanted to do, get away from the usual cliqued chord progressions of A, E, G, D that I had been using in The Sods. I wanted to add sharps and flats into the equation to make what I was playing sound more sinister; I just couldn't find a way to do it, it was so frustrating. I learnt all of the major chords, the minors, had even tried some of the diminished chords, still, every time I played around with a new riff, they just didn't sound right, then it all changed when I was down at Richard's house one night.

Richard had read in the Radio Times that Generation X were going to debut their new single 'King Rocker' on Top of the Pops, so we settled ourselves down to watch it with his old man, Pam, Andy his younger brother, and the two babies; Steven and David, who were building towers with building blocks and laughing uproariously when Andy knocked them down.

A poncy looking twat named Mike Read announced, "Now it's Generation X, aaaannnd King Rocker!"

Richard leant forward in his chair excitedly. "What is this? This is shit!" Richard said, pointing at the TV, a couple of bars into the track.

Steven and David froze, eyes like saucers looking at their cross older brother, his old man's head traversed to face him.

"Oh my god this is shit, Rock and Roll, why's he singing about Rock and Roll, we're Punks!"

"Richard!" His old man warned.

"It's shite though, crap, crap, crap!"

"If you're going to use language like that, I think it would be better if you go upstairs!"

Richard declared, "I'm not listening to this absolute shite." He jumped up and pounded out of the room, the babies' saucer like eyes tracking him all the way.

Andy grinned at me, I smiled back at him, stood up and left the room, following Richard up to his bedroom. Richard sat down heavily on his bed, picked up his bass, hammering into it.

"What a load of fucking shit, 'King Creole' that was the last generation, that's why they sang 'Your generation doesn't mean a thing to me'," he spat.

"I don't know Richard, I think that was the generation before, 'Your Generation', was an answer to The Who's track 'My Generation'," I said, joining him on his bed, picking up my guitar.

"I don't really care which generation it was, that was Rock and Roll rubbish, I can't believe it, why have they done that?"

"I don't know Rich; it wouldn't be the first punk band to go crap though would it, they all seem to sell out once they get famous."

Richard nodded sadly, head down, lashing into his bass strings, I grabbed a plectrum, joining in and one of our many jam sessions began. It wasn't loud enough for Richard, so he lurched forward, turned the volume up and then the bedroom door opened, so he jolted forward to turn it down and a grinning Andy walked into their shared bedroom.

"Dad's annoyed with you," he said, sitting down underneath his Charlie Harper poster above his bed, readjusting his long, peroxide blonde spiked-up hair.

Richard smirked at him and carrying on playing.

"Oh, is this a jam session?" Andy asked, "Can I play?"

Without waiting for an answer, he began playing 'Emotional Blackmail' by the UK Subs. It was perfect, sounded just like the track I knew and loved, so I stopped playing, watching as his hand dexterously moved up and down the threat board using just one chord, a chord I had never seen before.

"Andy, what's that you're playing there, mate?" I asked.

Andy stopped, looked up smiling, "Oh it's a bar chord, all the punk guitarist's use them," he explained coolly.

I nodded impressed.

"Here you are Skinner, this is bar E," Andy put his index finger across all of the guitar strings, trapping them, then with his other fingers he formed an E chord and began running the bar E chord up and down the guitar neck. Andy stopped on the third fret up, grinning at me like it was the easiest thing in the world.

"This is G, and if I slide down one fret it becomes F sharp or G flat."

I nodded, very impressed; it was exactly what I had been looking for, so I formed the chord myself, almost at once my hand cramped up.

"Ouch, Jesus that hurts' I said, shaking my aching hand.

Andy laughed knowingly back at me.

On the fifth attempt, I managed to hold the chord down, hearing only a few bum notes, so I began to slide it up and down the fret board like I had seen him do, after a while the ends of my fingers began to bleed like I had been sliding my fingers up and down cheese wire.

"Bloody hell, it's not the easiest chord to master, is it?" I complained.

"I can do it," Richard said, proudly.

I snorted, eyeing him, "I'm sure you can mate; you've got bass fingers."

"Richard's got old washer woman hands," Andy said, smiling at his older brother.

"That's a little bit harsh, isn't it?"

"Harsh realities of life, my friend," Andy returned.

"Bollocks," Richard said, finally.

Andy, Richard and me jammed until it was late, a soft tap on the door, told us how late it actually was, so Richard walked me to the door. Whilst we were talking on his doorstep, his old man strode past us on his way upstairs to bed, giving him discontented a look.

"I think I might be in trouble later," Richard laughed nervously to himself.

"Do you think so? I reckon I could beat my old man up; could you beat yours up?"

"No way," he said, shaking his head, furiously. "No, he's into keep fit, he does a bit of boxing."

"Street fighting's different, though, isn't it?"

Richard shook his head, "I don't know Skinner, I think fighting's, fighting. I saw him hit someone at a football match once."

I smiled at the thought of one of our dads having a punch up.

"I was playing, and some bloke swore at me for tackling his son, and my old man told him to leave it out, and he told my old man to piss off, so he decked him… Decked him with one punch, bam he was out on the floor, he's a decent fighter my old man."

"Oh what, he knocked him out!?"

Richard nodded proudly, "Well, he didn't get up again."

I creased up laughing, Richard joined in, and after we had said our goodbyes, I set off back to my house thinking that at last, I might be getting somewhere with the guitar.

A week of practising bar E and A, the cramping in my hand stopped and deep protective callouses formed on my fingertips, so with my hands now ready for action I set about putting a few riffs together; they sounded good. I loved the way I could mix up the flat with the sharp chords so easily. I could now use E, G, slip in an A sharp, which changed the whole cliqued E, G, A progression significantly, making it sinister, colder especially if it was played slowly. It was grinding, nasty, not only that it sounded fresh, new, like nothing I had heard before.

On top of that, I found that if I slid my fingers up or down the fret board, I could move the starting point of the first chord anywhere I wanted to, and I could use the same pattern of chords, it would always sound different. I wrote a whole bunch of riffs based on the E, G, A# progression – F, A #, B – C#, G, A#, and so on; it was the same, but it wasn't.

A whole new world of musical possibilities revealed themselves to me, I quickly worked out the death march chords of E, G, F# and once again I moved them, playing them in different combinations as I had with E, G, A# and again a new group of riffs revealed themselves to me.
In fact, I could use any group of chords in any combination, my only limitation now would be my imagination, I had plenty of ideas.

Chapter 4

C.J. Gets His Just (Sunshine) Desserts

I was on the right track with my music now, I couldn't say the same thing for school though, as my original feelings of frustration and boredom had steadily, with each passing week, turned into anger and resentment. I hated the old school tie mentality of Richard Hole, as we started calling it, the pettiness of it all was what I couldn't stand, the obsession with the uniform, which I soon modified with dozens of pin badges, and sixteen-hole DM's, to go with my spiked-up hair. I hated the cringing obedience that the teachers demanded, as far as I was concerned the majority of them were weaklings, sycophants who didn't deserve my respect, so to alleviate the boredom and make it more bearable, like many of the other kids in my year; the first comprehensive year, I acted up, revelling in mayhem.

One of our favourite pastimes was taking the piss out of everyone and everything mercilessly, no one was exempt, we all had our unflattering nicknames.

Richard was christened Rabbit or Watership Down as he had two large protruding front teeth, it didn't last long though, as he was superseded by his mate David Liddell who was even more bucktoothed. David Liddell was in a different class when it came to his gnashers, he was the super bunny, the true General Woundwort of the warren that was Richard Hole. It wasn't a problem, as someone noticed that Richard had a huge bottom lip like a fish, so we began calling him gudgeon, which mutated into Gudge-Gorm, Gudge as in piscine and Gorm as in gormless, eventually, we settled on The Gormless Gudgeon, which stuck for a while. It wasn't his worst name though and ironically it was his own fault that he had got it.

In a quiet moment, he had confessed to his close mate, Stephen Barnes, that when he was going out with a girl called Jenna Forwell, he had asked, 'I don't know how to kiss, can you teach us like?' Well, it didn't take long for Stephen to spread that gem around I can tell you. Stephen and me would see Richard pacing along the corridor towards us, get down on our knees, put our hands together like we were praying, pucker up and say, 'Oh please Jenna, teach me how to kiss' and we'd fall about laughing. One day, at first break whilst Stephen distracted him, I managed to draw a huge 'L' plate in chalk on his back, he didn't know anything about it, until someone told him as he got on the train to go home that evening; everyone must have seen it, even the teachers.

People say if you give it out, you should be able to take it back too, which I thought was fair enough. I had a big forehead, so Richard named me C.J. after the boss of Sunshine Desserts from the television show, The Fall and Rise of Reginald Perrin, who had a mountainous forehead. Richard would walk into our shared classes, come up to me, check his watch and say in his Reggie Perrin voice, 'Oh, morning C.J., sorry I'm late, burst water main at Kingston upon Thames,' sending everyone into hysterics. I had other names too, Blockhead was one, as I had made the fatal mistake of trying to cut my own hair in the classic Sid Vicious spike but had botched it so badly that it made my head look like a cube. It looked ridiculous, so after a few days of being called Michael Dury and the Blockhead, or Cuboid, I shaved it off to a number three and that was the end of the dreaded Cuboid.

I wasn't completely off the hook though, one day whilst Richard and me were sunning ourselves in some early spring sunshine, waiting to go into the gym, he noticed the shadow that my head was projecting onto the tarmac beneath us, particularly how my ears stuck out, so he rechristened me Cyberman, on the spot, which I didn't mind really, it was certainly better than Blockhead, or worse still the dreaded Cuboid. I never got angry about the names my mates called me as they were intended to be playful, a bit of fun to get us through the tedium of the day and certainly not hurtful. I thought we got off pretty lightly, really, as some of the other kids got far worse names than we did.

A kid in my form group called James Howe lived on a dairy farm, so with him living in such close proximity to all those lovely cows, it was only logical that we named him The Cow Fucker or 'Lord Jim of the order of Cow the Fuckers' on formal occasions. If that wasn't enough, poor Jim had a big nose too, so once again it was all about logic. I would ask Richard the logical question, 'Oi Richard, just how does Lord Jim of the order of the cow fuckers' fuck those cows?' and Richard's logical answer would be 'With his nose'.

James Fredley, another kid in my form group, probably got it the worst. Fred, as he was known before his rechristening, was a member of the first eleven rugby team and after matches, he would always shower in his underpants. Richard told me that the team were suspicious that he had no hair on his bollock sack so, they started calling him pubeless and then, just when he thought that things couldn't get any worse, the rugby team played against a first eleven from a little town in North Herts called Baldock and someone on the coach noticed that the sign for Baldock on the A505 had been altered to read 'Baldcock 5 Miles' and that was it, from that moment on James Fredley was known as Baldcock, or Baldcock 5 Inches.

It was only supposed to be a bit of fun, we were always pushing it though and inevitably sometimes we would go too far and if we saw someone taking it to heart, we would reign it in as we were mates, nobody wanted to fall out, particularly over some silly name-calling. I suppose when it came down to it, it was down to the individual and what they thought was acceptable, everybody had lines that they wouldn't cross and mine was racism, I couldn't stand it and didn't think there was any place for it, as far as I was concerned a black kid was just another kid at Richard Hole, who had to put up with the same shit that I had too. I saw racism at the school now and again; there was a kid in our year who used to hang out with us, he had black hair and a dark complexion, sometimes when he walked down the corridor at break time, some of the kids in our group would stick out their lips and say in an exaggerated Jamaican accent, 'hello der mon' laughing their heads off. I thought it was horrible, not only was it horrible, but it was also absolutely ridiculous as his old man was white and born in London and his mum came from Madrid, which is not a city in the Caribbean or African.

A couple of kids in our group who did it regularly seemed to think that taking the piss out of someone with a big hooter or a square head was the same as taking the piss out of the colour of someone's skin; it wasn't, they were being ignorant, they didn't know the history. I'll give him his due though, it never seemed to bother him, when the piss taking started, he would laugh and give it back to them as good as he was getting it; I hoped that when it came down to it, for most of the kids in our year, he was just another person in our circle of mates who took the piss out of each other and there was no real offence intended. It wasn't for me, though.

One red line we all shared was not letting kids outside our group use our piss taking names; that had to be nipped in the bud, or you could find the whole school was laughing at you, which would lead to a lack of respect, and inadvertently to fights; you could never let that happen.

On one occasion, I had heard from Andy that there was a kid in his form group, Martin 'Bunny' Hill, another one of the burgeoning rabbit population at Richard Hole, had been calling me blockhead in front of his mates to make himself look tough, getting some cheap laughs, at my expense so, I went straight down to have it out with him.

It was just before afternoon lessons were about to begin, his classroom was full of kids talking, laughing, getting their books out ready for the next lesson when I walked in. I saw Bunny Hills sitting at the back of the classroom and at first, he looked confused to see me marching towards him, then with a dawning realisation, his face turned ashen, his mouth gaping open, stupidly.

"I heard you been saying things about me?" I shouted.

Instantly it was silent in the classroom, all eyes on us.

Bunny Hills murmured, "No" shaking his head quickly.

I scowled and leant over his desk, he jolted backwards pushing down into his chair,

"Oh yeah, that's not what I heard, you fucking better not say anything again, bunny boy."

"I won't, I haven't, I didn't… I…"

I could see I had made my point; it still wasn't enough to quell my seething anger though, so I hawked up a huge bit of phlegm from my throat, spat it out onto his desk, turned and left, thinking good, no one in that class will ever hassle me again.

Mr. Clive 'Hair Bear' Harper, my history teacher, had already begun my first lesson of the afternoon, so I knocked on the door, apologised for being late and headed to my desk where I quickly got out my exercise book. A few moments later, I looked up to see Mr. Cecil 'Dr. White- The King of the Tampons', Bunny's form master, walk past the little window that connected my classroom to the corridor and thought… Oh shit.

Dr. White knocked on the grey door. He entered, pointing directly at me and motioned to Hair Bear Harper, "Oh hello, I need Baker."

Hair Bear Harper gave me a cursory glance, nodding in the affirmative, and I walked out of the classroom with twenty-five pairs of mirthful eyes burning into the back of my neck.

Once I was in the corridor Dr. White said, "The headmaster wants to see you," in a dour tone.

Dr. White 'The King of the Tampons' set off at a brisk pace in silence, I fell into step behind him, our footsteps echoing down the now empty corridor. I knew I was in trouble as our Headmaster Mr. Dennis F. Jack 'Jack the Whack' had a formidable no-nonsense reputation when it came to discipline and a swing to match, hence his moniker. I had first-hand knowledge of this from my second year, after a pre-Baldcock Fred and me had been caught cheating at cross-country running, it had been so easy to take the shortcut. Unfortunately for us though, we had come back too early and cut a full two minutes off the world record for five miles.

Dr. White knocked on Jack the Whack's door and opened it a crack. I felt the butterflies in my stomach building up to a crescendo and pawed at my chin with a shaky hand.

"I've got Baker here, sir," Dr. White said, indicating for me to go in.

I shuffled in, the door banged shut ominously behind me, I took a deep breath. In front of me by the window, next to a huge brown radiator sat Jack the Whack, straight-backed behind his desk, wearing his usual full dress robes and a mortar board hat balanced on his head. Jack the Whack looked up, observing me for a while, taking his time, building up the suspense.

"Sit down, Baker," he said, eventually.

I complied.

"I've been told that you spat on another pupil's desk. Is this true?" He said, in a measured tone.

I swallowed hard, "Yes, sir."

"Why did you do that, Baker?" He asked.

"Err… He called me names, sir," I replied.

Jack the Whack nodded thoughtfully and stood up, draping his robe onto the back of his chair.

"I'm sorry I have to do this."

I knew what was coming, I couldn't look, so I stared at the beautiful blue sky out of the window above the radiator while he turned and opened a small cupboard, which held his selection of canes. My eyes involuntarily pulled away from the blue, I saw him select two, gauge them individually between his finger and thumb like a professional tradesman, then finding the correct tool for the job he placed the other one back into the cupboard for safe keeping.

Jack the Whack moved in front of my blue sky, blocking my only escape, now only a silhouette in front of the large sash window above the radiator.

"Come here, please," he said, emotionlessly.

I felt a flash of fear shoot through me and hesitantly moved towards him, hanging back, trying to delay the inevitable.

Jack the Whack instructed, "Bend over." His voice bereft of any sort of humanity.

I thought OK here it comes, whatever you do, don't call out. I bent forward, placed my hands onto the radiator and instantly recoiled, almost shouting out loud before the first blows fell. It was scolding hot. I put my stinging hands to my side, bracing myself. Jack the Whack took six straight-armed swings at me, which I hardly felt as my hands were throbbing so badly, I was in agony. Jack the Whack stepped back, nodding to himself satisfied, mistaking my grimacing face for his work; it wasn't, I was thinking about skin grafts.

I stood up, furiously rubbing my hands together, and he placed the fit for the purpose cane back into the cupboard, closing the door with a severe click.

Jack the Whack sat back behind his desk, weaving his arms back into his robe.

"You can go now, Baker, and I don't want to see you in here again," he said solemnly.

I thought that didn't hurt a bit, you silly old sod, so I grinned and said, "Thank you," pleasantly.

Jack the Whack smiled back, "Thank..." then his smile dropped like a stone.

I smiled at the old fool again, making my way to the door, his head swivelling like a bird of prey watching my every move, his face caught somewhere between furious anger and cold shock at the audacity of this cheeky little yob in front of him. I closed the door behind me and strutted off down the corridor, thinking I can't wait to tell everyone about this; he's lost his strength in his right arm, Jack's lost his whack. I couldn't believe it, the last time I had the cane from him, I had deep welts on my arse for weeks afterwards. I grinned and thought, the only marks I'm going to have after whatever that was supposed to be are on my hands. I put them up in front of my face, examining the glowing red areas, and quickly made my way to the toilets to splash some icy cold water on them. Not long afterwards, 'Jack the Whack' was renamed 'Whackless Jack'.

Chapter 5

The Frog and Breeze Block

In the fourth year at Richard Hole school, pupils were deemed responsible enough to go down into Hertford town at dinner break, which was great for us. It felt like we were free, we could go anywhere, do anything we liked, there would be no more sneaking off behind the pavilion on the top field for a crafty fag anymore; we had the whole of Hertford to smoke in now. I used to go to Richard's house most days after school, so I would usually get the train back to Ware with him, spend a couple of hours jamming, and then walk the two miles back to mine. It was cheaper than the bus fare, so with the saved money from that, plus my dinner money, I would have a few quid to spend on more important things like fags and chips. Once the dinner bell rang, most days, we would go to the Sunshine Garden Chinese restaurant, get a couple of bags of chips with sweet and sour sauce, then wander over into the main town, sometimes eating the chips but mostly, we would eat them until the pot of sweet and sour source had gone, then chuck the rest at each other. On-the-go lunch completed, we would carry on to the local independent record shop franchise, Tracks.

Tracks was great, we loved it, we would read about the new releases in Sounds or hear something on John Peel and more often than not, Tracks would have it in. If we hadn't heard of anything new coming out, we would still have a look, as the covers of all the new punk release singles were blue tacked up onto the wall behind the counter. If we liked the look of anything and if the guy who worked there, Bone, was in a good mood, he would play them for us and more often than not, we would like what we heard; there was nothing quite like that feeling we had when we discovered a new band, sometimes it felt like we were finding buried treasure.

Once we had checked the new releases in Tracks, we would saunter on down through Bull Plain out onto folly island, where we would walk up the tow-path alongside the river Lee, passing Richard's real mum's house, our final destination being the viaduct where the Herford East railway line crosses the Lee on its way to Liverpool Street. It was the perfect meeting point for the fourth and fifth years as it was quiet, out of the way.

One Friday afternoon, instead of going to the last three periods of the day games, with Roger 'Lovely Boys Boy Hopper' Hopkins and his sidekick, Peter 'Jam Rolly Polly' James, Richard, Stephen Barnes and me went to the viaduct and found a lot of kids standing around in groups smoking and larking about, who didn't fancy games that afternoon either. In one of the groups, stood Sean 'Bean' Beresford who dossed me out as soon as he saw me approaching, I held his gaze, wondering what he was looking at, then I remembered.

I had some trouble with him back in the second year, thought it was over with, but the look he was giving me now told me he hadn't forgotten.

Bean was a big bloke, liked to show it too. At break times, he would walk down the middle of the corridor, shoulder-barging kids who were walking in the opposite direction, out of the way, most of the time the kids wouldn't even know what had hit them. One minute they would be strolling along quite happily talking to their mates, or in deep thought, then, BAM, they would be on the floor, dazed, looking up at the ceiling, which is exactly what had happened to me. I had dusted myself down, got up and sworn to myself that I would be ready for him next time. A few days later I got my chance, Bean was marching aggressively towards me, so I looked out of the window into the playground, pretending to wave to a mate, acting like I hadn't noticed him coming, then at the last moment when he was inches away, I span, ramming into him so hard that he went down on his arse. I smirked down at him and carried on, on my way.

I nodded at Bean, he nodded back, nudging the kid standing next to him, Steve Minter, supposedly the hardest kid in the school, who stared sourly in my direction. I held his stare, watching as he took a puff from his fag, blew out a pillar of white smoke and spat on the ground. It suddenly dawned on me that staring at Steve Minter probably wasn't a good idea, I looked away.

Stephen Barnes was a mate of Steve Minter, so before I could say anything, he greeted his almost namesake with a wankers sign and strode over to join him. I glanced at Richard; he shrugged his shoulders, and we followed Stephen over to the group, who were in rapt conversation about one of our chemistry teachers. Mr. Alfred 'Bagpuss' Bagley, apparently he had been caught stealing butter out of Woolworths in the town centre. Steve Minter said it was true as one of his mates, Paul 'Jack' Frost, had witnessed him being taken away by the filth.

Stephen grinned, tapping ash off his fag, "I've got Bagley first period tomorrow, I'm going to bring some butter in and leave it on his desk, see what he says."

Steve Minter laughed, "Yeah, nice one… That would piss him off, the silly old bastard."

"I reckon he would take it home with him, Bagley loves free butter," I said, joining in.

Steve Minter eyed me for a moment, shook his bald head and passed his fag to Bean who took a huge toke on it, holding the smoke down.

"You want some?" Asked Bean, seeing my puzzled face.

"What is it?" I asked.

Bean snorted, "It's grass." Holding it out to me.

"OK," I said, taking a deep lug on it, holding it down like I had just watched him do.

I felt a calming warmth spread throughout my body, all of a sudden, the river Lee seemed to be a lot bluer than it had been a few moments ago.

"Hmmm that's nice," I said, handing it to Richard.

Richard took a couple of half-hearted pulls on it, then handed it back to the smirking Bean, who took a couple of drags on it himself, before dobbing it out on a huge stack of breeze blocks, which stood pyramid like next to him.

I continued, "Bagley... We should rename him Butter Bagley," and everyone creased up.

"Yeah, I like it Butter Bagley, the Butter Bandit," Stephen riffed.

"Butter Bandit Bagley," said Bean, grinning lopsidedly.

A loud hysterical laugh rang out from one of the other groups of kids underneath the viaduct, taking our attention away from our

Bagley Baiting, so just for a laugh Bean theatrically picked up one of the breeze blocks, from the stack and chucked it in their direction. The grey stone block twisted twice in the air and bounced past the group, who immediately fell silent.

One of the group, James 'Baldcock' Fredley, walked over towards us.

"Oi, be careful with that," he said, eyeing Bean.

"What, you mean these?" Bean retorted, hoisting another one up high above his head menacingly.

Fred paused, looking on the ground near the stack, then eyes wide with fascination he pointed, "Oh, look it's a frog. It must have been hiding under there; it must be its home."

I smirked and picked up one of the blocks, holding it high above my head as a joke, pretending that I was going to drop it on top of the frog.

Steve Minter chanted, "Do it, do it, do, it…" Soon everybody joined in.

"DO IT! DO IT! DO IT! DO IT! DO IT! DO IT! DO IT!" The viaduct echoed.

In amongst the sound of the baying kids, I could hear another sound building, a train was approaching, fast. It thundered over the top of us, making the viaduct shake.

"DO IT! DO IT! DO IT! DO IT! DO IT! DO IT! DO IT!"

I realised I had made a mistake; I had painted myself into a corner, it was either me or the frog. I tentatively looked at Steve Minter, who smirked, giving me the Roman thumbs down sign.

"DO IT! DO IT! DO IT! DO IT! DO IT! DO IT! DO IT…"

I nodded and smashed the grey block down, crushing the frog beneath it. My audience cheered their approval. I sniffed loudly and kicked the block off to check my handy work. In amongst the mud, blood, distended organs, the frog's lifeless eyes looked up at me accusingly. I felt a push at my shoulder, Bean and Steve Minter had joined me.

"Eerrgh look at its guts," Bean said, prodding the frog, mud and mush with his foot.

I heard a cry and looked up to see Fred, tears filling his eyes.

"Oh, that was a horrible thing to do, Baker, horrible."

"Fuck off Baldcock," I snapped back at the soppy twat.

The viaduct echoed with laughter.

"Why don't you go and grow some fucking pubes Bald dick?" I added, enjoying the adulation.

Bean chortled, "What are you blubbing about, Baldcock? Aww, is it one of your relatives?"

"Yeah, fuck off, freddo the frog," Steve Minter said, finally.

A sobbing Baldcock trudged out from under the viaduct, all of us jeering him as he went.
Richard and me hung around for a while longer, smoking some normal cigarettes with our new mates, chatting, pissing about, then after saying our 'see you laters' we strolled back along the River Lee together, back towards Hertford town centre.

"I'm not smoking grass again, it's for junkies," said Richard.

I nodded my head, thinking that I might give it another try one day, I was still feeling that warmth and the River Lee looked absolutely fascinating.

"It's a beautiful day, isn't it?" I said, focusing on the azure river.

Richard laughed, "Yeah it is. Where shall we go now?"

I smiled broadly, "Tracks?" I ventured.

Richard nodded his head in the affirmative.

Once we had passed Richard's mum's house, the spires and rooftops of Hertford town centre came into view, spreading out before us, in a glow of terracotta.

I turned my attention back to the undulating azure waters of the River Lee. Up ahead, Mike Barker and another kid from Richard Hole, were trying to rescue a football from the river, the current was not making it easy, as it slowly wafted the ball along the water's edge. It wasn't going to get the better of Mike Barker that was for sure, he ran down the bank, reaching out, then just as his fingers grazed over the top of the ball, it span away further down the bank, Mike moved along with it, stretching perilously over the water.

Richard and me nodded at the other kid, I wandered down the bank.

"I'll help," I said, reaching out my hand.

"Oh, cheers, Baker," Mike replied, gratefully grabbing my hand. Once the grip was tight, he looked back across the water to see where that pesky ball was.

Mike reached out as far as he could and got some purchase on the ball, tentatively he began to flip it towards him, sending gentle ripples across the water. I grinned at Richard, let his hand go, and he toppled forwards, arms flailing madly, trying to balance himself, then with a split-second decision of either going into the water head-first or feet-first, he made the right decision and jumped feet first into the river. Mike spun around, glaring at Richard and me, we both cracked up laughing at him as he stood knee-deep in the river Lee, then once we had stopped laughing, we nonchalantly walked on up towards the spires and rooftops of Hertford town.

Richard and me spent the rest of the supposed school day hanging around in Tracks, listening to the new punk releases, which was a lot better than sweating our bollocks off running around the top field being shouted at by fat teachers, 'Lovely Boys, Boy Hopper', and 'Jam Rolly Polly', for being unfit, even more so as Bone was in good mood that day, playing us any single from the wall, we wanted him to.

A group of Richard Hole kids entered Tracks, which told us that it was safe to break cover, so we left Tracks, making our way to Hertford East station to get the train to Ware.

On arrival at the station, our train was already on the platform, so we legged it up to a carriage near the back of the train, pulled open its heavy doors and found ourselves a couple of seats.
Inside it was absolutely baking, even with the sliding windows in the doors fully down, it must have been touching thirty degrees.

Dave 'General Woundwort' Liddell the super bunny ran past by our window.

"RUN RABBIT, RUN RABBIT, RUN, RUN, RUN!" Richard shouted, curling his hands into paws, sticking out his already protruding front teeth.

Dave gave us a toothy smile and carried on.

A few minutes passed, and we heard a door crash shut, and the train started to move, then with a hiss from the hydraulic brakes and a huge creak, it abruptly stopped, jarring us forwards in our seats.

"Oh, fucking hell. What's going on? It's too hot for this," Richard said.

"I don't know, Rich," I said, wiping at my feverish brow.

I had never felt this kind of heat before, it felt even hotter in the carriage than when we had first got in, the oppressive heat was building by the minute.

Richard sighed and pushed his hand through his short blonde spikes, "I bet it's Peter Pearman, I saw him up ahead of us. I bet he's had another one of his epileptic fits."

"Yeah mate, sure it is," I replied, sarcastically, scratching my chin like he was bullshitting.

"It could be Skin, he had one a few days ago when we were playing football on the tennis courts, it was sweltering that day too."

"I heard something about that... What happened?"

"One minute he was running about, the next he was rolling around on the floor, all gob coming out of his mouth, I went to get help, and it was only Bagley on lunch duty, wasn't it... You know what he's like, he starts running around like Jonesy off Dad's army, he's like, don't panic, don't panic, don't panic! The silly old twat."

"Bloody hell, I'm surprised Pearman survived."

Richard grinned, "Me too, they should sack Bagley, he's rubbish."

I snorted, "Sack Bagley, there's a joke in there somewhere."

He laughed, "Bagley is the joke."

"You know Alistair Campbell?"

Richard nodded, "What the posh twat with the briefcase, who pretends to be Scottish?"

"Yeah, that's him."

"Ooh eye der now, where's me scaff, why yon," Richard Alistair Campbell-ed in his nowhere near Scottish accent. "It's nothing like it, the wazzock," he added.

"I was in his chemistry class in the first year, we had Butter Bagley, and for some stupid reason he kept calling Campbell, Camp. Bell. Like it was some kind of double-barrelled name," I said, cracking up.

"Oh, good morning, Camp. Bell. Have you got an apple for teacher today?" I Bagley-ed.

"Camp. Bell." Richard repeated, laughing.

"You know what. I reckon he got it right, he missed the end off though," I laughed.

"What? I don't get it," Richard said, confused.

"Camp Bell End." I quipped.

Richard creased up.

"First to class, first to put his hand up, last to leave class, and last to try to light one of the gas taps up," I said, continuing my Camp Bell autopsy.

Richard and me dissolved into fits of laughter, throwing ourselves back onto the grilling heat of faux leather on the seats.

Richard sighed, rubbing at his thigh self-consciously, "Did you know Bagley pulled a tea urn over me when I was in second year?"

"What? Fucking hell, no, I didn't!"

"Yeah, it was in the new cafeteria. I was standing behind him in the queue to get some tea, and he pulled the tap sideways on the tea urn, and it fell over, the tea went all over my leg."

"Jesus Christ, what did you say?"

"Aaaaahhhhhhhhhhh!"

I smirked, "Oh, OK yeah very good... No seriously, what did you say?"

Richard laughed, "I shouted, 'you stupid old bastard' and you know what, that little Gestapo officer, Greg Young, runs over and says, 'Well there is no need for that kind of language'."

I exhaled sharply, placing my face in my hands, "Oh what!? So your legs are covered in boiling hot tea, burning up like molten lava and all he's worried about is your language... Fucking hell, it just about sums this place up, doesn't it...? Bagley, he really is a stupid old bastard, isn't he? They should sack Bagley."

"Bag Sackley, chuck him in the river with Mike Barker," said Richard, finding the joke in there.

I laughed, pulling an exercise book from my bag and waving it in front of my face in a futile attempt to cool down, "I can't take much more of this."

"Oh my god..." said Richard, mouth open, gaping out of the window.

A group of paramedics rushed past, pushing a gurney with Peter Pearman secured tightly to it, mouth dribbling, his eyes red, blazing, staring vacantly into space.

I opened my mouth to say something, found I had nothing to say, so I just wiggled my fingers in Richard's face, humming the theme tune to the Twilight Zone, sending us both into hysterics.

Once Peter Pearman had been taken off the platform and safely loaded into an ambulance for transportation, the train moved off, headed out of the station, and onto the open track ahead. As it picked up speed, thumping noisily over the sleepers, gusts of cool air rushed in through the open windows, pushing the stifling heat out of the carriages. I smiled to myself and jumped up, leaning out of the open window on the door, embracing the sweet cooling wind on my face, I breathed it all in, watching the deep green fields rush by. Richard was on the other side of the carriage doing exactly the same, drinking it in, cooling down, reviving, feeling better, enjoying the momentum of the speeding train.

A horn blared out, alerting other trains of our presence at the junction with the River Lee viaduct, the scene of my earlier crime, I felt ashamed of myself for killing the poor frog. It hadn't done me any harm; it was just living its life; it had looked cute before I had mashed its helpless body into the ground. I told myself to shut up, pushed the image of its tiny, mangled limbs out of my mind, opened my eyes, and got back to enjoying the journey.

The train began to slow as it came into Ware station, sounding its horn again, hydraulic brakes hissing, the front end speeding past the platform. I pulled the latch down on the carriage's heavy outer door and immediately, the door swung backwards in the pushing wind caused by the train's momentum, crashing onto the side of the carriage. A massive shot of adrenaline rushed through me as I watched the racing tarmac beneath my feet. I steeled myself and jumped out, hitting the ground running, running as fast as I could, before smoothly slowing down to a walk.

I chuckled to myself and looked back at the still moving train.

Richard jumped out of the carriage and tumbled forward, going straight down on his face, staying there, not moving. I ran over, worried for my mate.

"Bloody hell, are you alright, Rich?"

"Yeah," he replied, uncertainly, rubbing at the back of his head furiously.

"Ouch… That fucking hurts," he said, holding up a blood soaked hand, inspecting it.

"Jesus, Rich, let's have a look," I said, my voice full of concern.

Richard flipped his hand over, revealing a deep two-inch slice on his palm. He took a deep breath, laughed and shook his head, like now he had seen it, he was dismissing it.

"Oh shit, that's bad, mate," I said, my voice still full of concern.

"I'm fine."

"Don't worry, C.J. it's just a flesh wound," he joked in his Reggie Perrin voice.

I laughed, "OK Reggie, if you're sure," I C.J.-ed back.

"Yes, yes, yes, er… Sorry C.J., eleven minutes late, some spac jumped off the train and landed on his face," in full Reggie Perrin mode now.

I creased up, "OK, don't milk it, Jenna."

"Sorry C.J."

"Oh please, Jenna, can you teach me how to jump off a train," I Richard-ed back at him, sending us both into fits of laughter.

Richard rubbed some of the drying blood off his hands and looked over towards the turnstiles, pointed at Dave Liddell's retreating form.

"Look, there's the wanking rabbit."

"Oi! Bugs Bunny!" He shouted.

Dave Liddell turned around, giving us a toothy grin before walking into the station building slowly shaking his head, with us following behind.

I was relieved to see there wasn't a ticket inspector on duty at the turnstiles, as I had been flashing the same ticket all week. If the inspectors were in the mood to do some work, which wasn't that often, they would check, not today though. I kissed my golden ticket extravagantly and put it back into my pocket for next time, smirking self-indulgently at Richard, who in turn nodded back, also returning his golden ticket to his pocket and laughing together at the incompetents of British Rail, we walked straight through the barrier, out of the station building.

Dave was waiting for us and gave Richard a playful kick up the arse.

"Blockhead! Jenna!" He said, his face breaking into a huge grin.

Richard grinned back, "Major Woundwort, I presume?"

Richard and Dave Liddell knew each other well, they played in the notorious first eleven rugby team together. I didn't really know Dave and on the occasions that we had met, he seemed a bit aloof, not interested in talking to me, so I stood back listening as Richard told Dave about our afternoon's adventures.

I noticed Dave was holding a yellow bag with Tracks written on the side of it in black italics.

"What you got?" I asked, pointing at the bag.

"Buzzcocks, Another Music in a Different Kitchen," Dave replied proudly.

"Oh what, I got that. It's brilliant, isn't it?"

Dave nodded, opened the bag, "If you like that, you'll love this." He pulled out The Dead Kennedy's album 'Fresh Fruit for Rotting Vegetables'.

"I didn't know you were into Punk, Dave," I exclaimed.

Dave smiled patiently, "I like some of it, Siouxsie and the Banshees, Generation X, Dead Kennedys, Buzzcocks they're all good, I've got most of their singles, I like The Clash the best though, those first two albums are amazing."

I thought, bloody hell, I didn't know that. Anyone who's into Punk is alright with me, so together the three of us walked up into Ware town centre.

Chapter 6

Where Am I? You Are in The Village

I lived in a village called Thundridge, which we unimaginatively named The Village, it was a couple of miles north of Ware, where Richard lived. If we hadn't spent too much time in Tracks or messing about on the trains, on the way home some days, instead of going to his house, we would stroll up to the village, see what my mates were up to.

Richard was friendly, outgoing, a good laugh, so it didn't take him long to fit in with my mates in the village. Once they had met him a few times, because of his spiked up blonde hair they started calling him Billy Idol; after a while everyone in the village called him Billy Idol, even my old man started calling him it, which Richard found hilarious.

A couple of weeks after Richard had first set foot in the village, Diane Hyde, one of the local girls, took a shine to him, they started going out together. It worked out perfectly for me, as she was best mates with my girlfriend, Clare Jonas, as they used to ride their ponies together, so we double dated them. With regard to the girls, it was great living out in the village as we could walk out into the fields, find a nice quiet spot and do as much as the girls would let us do. Most of the time, they were well up for it; we certainly enjoyed a few teenage kicks with them.

If we weren't out in the fields rolling around with the girls or hanging around the village with our mates, chain-smoking and spitting on the pavements, we would be back at mine practising, jamming or going through some of the new guitar riffs that I had written. I had also started writing lyrics again. Gone were the childish meanderings of The Sods, I wrote material of a more political nature now: religions, governments, the police and the military were my main targets. I was angry, angry with the world, that anger spilled over, manifesting itself in my lyrics and the aggressive style of music I had begun to write would give them the perfect platform.

I was under no illusions, I lived in a nice house in a nice village, some of the things I had read in the newspapers though, and seen on the TV over the years, had shown me a different world. A world where people were suffering unnecessary at the hands of the very people who should have been there to look after them - the fascists, the communists, the totalitarian religious states and monarchies of the world, all clamping down on the people of their countries by breaking their minds or if they couldn't do that, breaking their bodies.

In comparison, my problems were small, but I didn't think my experience of the society I lived in had been a good one either. I hated school, as far as I was concerned education was a ruse, a way of brainwashing us all into being good little citizens, so we could carry on making lots of money for the rich and powerful, to keep them in the style they had become accustomed to. If we had the audacity to question them, or worse still, refuse, then the police, 'the army of the rich' would only be so happy to show us the error of our ways by smashing our fucking skulls in. I had a deep knowledge of politics for someone of my age, as my old man was obsessed with them and from a very young age he would, what he called 'debate me', which was basically him droning on about someone who said this, or someone who didn't say that; it bored me to death. In the end, I found the only way to stop the ranting avalanche of reactionary right-wing politics was to say something contradictory back, which often led to furious arguments, until my mum stepped in, to calm things down. I'll say this for the old man, even though his inane rambling drove me to distraction, he was certainly inspirational, he made me think. Once I had thought the subject through, I made up my own mind, and now with my music and lyrics, I had the perfect outlet to say what I thought on the matter.

In the weeks following the demise of The Sods, I started thinking of a name for the new band, I already had the logo, a jawless skull sitting on a V, which I had nicked from a story called 'Invasion' in the comic 2000AD, so it had to begin with a V. I found the letter 'V' symbolic as the 'V sign' had several connotations, it said 'peace', it said 'victory' and it said 'stick it up your arse', which were all fundamental to punk. I liked the skull too, the way it sat edgily on top of the V. It was a stirring image, menacing, strong and powerful, which I thought would be a good indication of our music and our message.

Once I had this, the band name, Virus, soon followed. It was a simple choice as far as I was concerned; punk was like a disease, as it spread, it infected people, waking them from their slumber, although some couldn't handle it, others heard the call, and it made them stronger, resilient, more knowledgeable about the lies that surrounded them - it was basically, kill or cure, depending on your taste in music and general world view. I added the V1 later, after seeing a band called the Virus in Sounds, just to make sure there was no mistake about who was who.

Virus V1 was born, we had some decent ideas for tracks and plenty of enthusiasm to go with it, now to complete the circle we needed a drummer and a singer; we needed them now.

In keeping with the idea of getting my mates into the band, I didn't have too far to look for our drummer. Dave Williams had gone to Thundridge J.M.I school, or The Junior Mental Institution as we called it, he was a close mate, someone I could trust and most importantly he was always up for a laugh. Dave and me had only stopped seeing each other when he went to a different secondary school to me, Fanshawe or Shit-Shores, as it was known locally. I hadn't seen him for a couple of years, then one day we bumped into each other outside the local shop, we started talking. Dave had grown a lot in the intervening years, he had shot up to well over six-feet-tall and his once blonde, curly hair had darkened some. I had changed too - ripped T-shirt, safety pins, drainpipe trousers, left ear pierced with a metal compass from school, my hair had got lighter, under the fizz of half a bottle of peroxide. Both of us may have looked different, but the more we talked, it became obvious that we were still on the same wavelength. Dave was still as mad as he ever was so, when he asked me to come around for him, I didn't hesitate and since then, we had been causing absolute chaos.

One of our favourite pastimes was to lob stones at people whilst they filled up their cars at the local, all-night petrol station on the A10, the main road that ran through the village. Once the cashiers had gone home, the pumps became completely automated, all the patrons needed to do to get the precious juice was to slide their, not too crumpled five-pound notes, into the side of one of the pumps, and hey presto, they could fill up their empty tanks. It was as easy as that... Unless we were about.

In the hours after darkness fell, Dave and me would hide behind one of the huge cypress trees that ran alongside a small gravel track, that led up to the graveyard, on the opposite side of the road, waiting for an unsuspecting victim.

On one such night, a dark Ford Escort pulled up at the station, a short fat bloke in overalls got out, fed his fiver into the pump, pulled out the hose and began filling his car up. I looked at Dave's eyes glinting mischievously back at me.

"You ready?" I asked.

Dave nodded; he was always ready.

I chucked a stone about the size of a golf ball towards the garage, watching it disappearing into the darkness.

KIK KIk, Kik, kik, kik… It skimmed across the concrete near Fat Ford bloke. He froze.

A few silent moments passed, and Dave threw one, again it disappeared into the darkness, and we grimaced, waiting for it to hit home.

BAM… It struck the corrugated iron roof above the forecourt.

Fat Ford bloke ducked down onto his haunches, his head swivelling frantically from left to right, trying to make out what the fucking hell was going on.

Dave and me watched, laughing our heads off at the poor sap, waiting for him to settle down, keeping it subtle to begin with, seeing how he reacted. Fat Ford bloke tentatively straightened up, his head still swivelling left then right, and gingerly got back to filling his car up.

KIK KIk, Kik, kik, kik… Another stone skated across the forecourt sending Fat Ford blokes head spinning in every direction.

"OI! PACK IT IN!" He shouted.

BAM! BAM! BAM! Stones bounced off the corrugated iron above his head.

"I DON'T KNOW WHO YOU ARE, BUT YOU BETTER PACK IT IN NOW!"

It was time... The perfect moment to unleash hell. We let loose a whole barrage of stones, which flew off disappearing into the chilly dark night, raining down onto the garage like hail, skipping across the concrete forecourt, ricocheting off the corrugated iron roof in a tumult.

"YOU LITTLE BASTARDS!"

Fat Ford bloke dived for cover behind his car, and we launched a second barrage, which also scored direct hits on all of its intended targets.

KIK KIk, Kik, kik, kik... BAM, BAM, BAM...KIK Kik, kik, kik... BAM, BAM, BAM!

In amongst the maelstrom of flint, granite and chert, there was a series of sharp metallic 'tangs' as some of the stones rebounded off fat Ford bloke's dark Ford escort, then... Silence.

Dave and me waited for the final part of the game to begin; it could go two ways, the victim would either jump in his car and get the hell out of there, or......

Fat Ford bloke's head popped up above his bonnet, he was looking directly at us. He took his chance, made a run for the driver's door, pulled it open, jumped in, turned the motor over and floored it.

In a second, the dark fiesta screeched off the forecourt, wheels spinning, across the main road and powered up the hill towards us, headlights blazing.

Dave and me legged it as fast as we could, as we entered the graveyard, our shadows danced, erratically, over the gravestones in the glare of Fat Ford bloke's high beams.

I stopped by the wall at the edge of the graveyard to give our pursuer the wankers sign, and Dave piled into the back of me, laughing like a mad bastard.

"Come on, Skin, this wanker's a live one!" he grinned.

I cackled back at him, in unison, like crazed synchronised gymnasts we vaulted the wall, and ran full pelt into 'the pit', a patch of waste ground behind my house, to lie low for a while.

Once we had got our breaths back and stopped laughing, I mentioned to Dave that Richard and me were getting a punk band together, we were looking for a drummer and a singer.

"Oh, nice one, that's a great idea," he said enthusiastically.

I told him what kind of music we would be playing, the message we hoped to put across, and without hesitation, he said that he was interested, that he had always wanted to learn how to play the drums and this would give him a good reason to start. Dave said he would talk to his parents about it, ask them if he could get a drum kit and set it up in his bedroom. I knew that their bedroom was right next to his. I can't see that happening, I thought cynically.

A car tooted loudly in the distance, disturbing us from our conversation, reminding us of why we were lying low in the first place. It must have been at least half an hour since the stoning of Fat Ford bloke, a man who went straight in at number three of our all-time top ten stone-ees for his brilliant reaction. It was almost time to break cover.

"You reckon it's safe yet?" I ventured.

Dave laughed, "I don't know, he was a mad one wasn't he, let's take a slow walk back, you never know."

I smiled back, knowingly, maybe we should stop this, I thought, it's pretty stupid stoning people at an all-night garage, which is right next to Dave's house.

A few weeks later, Dave told me excitedly that his parents had given him the green light, he was getting a set of drums. I still wasn't sure whether to believe him or not, then a couple of days later, when I went around for him, his older sister Hayley let me into the house. I could hear him up in his bedroom knocking out a stuttering beat.

Hayley said, "I think you know where he is, Skinner," a smile playing at her full lips.

I nodded, rushed past her, upstairs to his bedroom, and there he was, sitting behind a white pearl premier drum kit, beaming at me.

"I told you, Skin, I told you!"

"Brilliant, it's fucking brilliant Dave, what a beautiful kit mate."

Dave knocked out a jaunty beat and hit a drum roll, dropping one of his sticks, which flew off onto the window with a crack.

"Yeah, well it might take me a while to be any good," Dave laughed, getting up to retrieve it.

"Oh, don't worry about it mate; you've got plenty of time, we are all practising, and we've still got to get a singer."

"I love this, I'll practice every chance I get!"

Once he'd retrieved it, he sat down, lurched forward on his stool, tensed his arms, tried the roll again, again and kept on trying for the rest of the evening; even as I left, he was still going at it.

I thought that's just the kind of spirit we need in the band, we don't need musicians, we don't need posers, we don't need wankers, we need people who want to give it a go, if it didn't come easily, so what, we would just have to keep on trying until it did.

Dave was holding down a beat within a few days, his drum rolls were coming along nicely too, so to help him on his way, give him an idea of the kind of music we would be playing, I lent him 'Why' by Discharge, 'Punks not Dead' by The Exploited and the two E.P.s by Rudimentary Peni, who he took to immediately. Rudimentary Peni, were the perfect punk band to play along with as far as Dave was concerned, he told me, he loved how varied the tracks were, some fast, others slow, and that their drummer Jon Greville was brilliant, right on the money, on every one of them. They soon became his favourite band, he told me that most days he would give the 'Farce' E.P. a spin, even if he wasn't practising along to it.

Chapter 7

The Thief, The Voyeur and The Brother

I had now recruited two of my mates into the band and had three people in mind for our vocalist, unfortunately, only one of them, Barry 'Basher' Argyle, I would have classed as a mate. I had met him when I was hanging out in Hertford Heath with Chris Almond, a fellow inmate of Richard hole school, and we had hit it off straight away. Basher looked perfect, he had a Mohican and wore green, tartan bondage trousers. Not only was he into punk, he loved his snooker too, so some weekends he would walk the five miles up to mine to play on my mini snooker table. Basher and me would have some mega snooker sessions lasting six, sometimes eight hours. With a 'home table' advantage, I would usually beat him by some ridiculous old school snooker score of something like thirty-three to twenty-two.

Basher was impressed with our lyrics, he told me that they reminded him of his favourite band, Conflict's lyrics, also if we were auditioning people, he would be well up for it, love to give it a go, and in turn I told him that I would let him know. I thought we might have found our man here, Basher had a problem though, he was a complete kleptomaniac. Basher would nick anything, any time, and he was good at it too. I thought it was hilarious when he came out of shops, swept open his jacket like a flasher, to reveal a bounty of sweets and chocolate bars, he even nicked a packet of tampons once and wandered around Hertford town centre wearing them like earrings, which cracked me up. However, my laughter soon turned into anger when my Crass - The Feeding of the Five Thousand album, the rare, first sitting, disappeared.

I loved the album, since its release in 1979, I had almost played the grooves flat on it, then when their second album 'Stations of The Crass' came out, I put 'Feeding' aside and did exactly the same thing, until one day I fancied giving it a spin again. I looked in my record box… I couldn't find it, it was gone. I turned my bedroom upside down looking for it, which wasn't totally fruitless, as I had found an old Lurker's single jammed under my wardrobe, no Crass album though. I asked my mates if I leant it to one of them. I knew I hadn't, so it was no surprise when they shrugged their shoulders, looking at me like I was losing it. At the time, I thought they might be right. It was driving me mad, so I sat down to think, trying to work it out and slowly but surely, it all began to make sense.

Basher and me had been up in my bedroom listening to music on my record player, taking a break from one of our marathon snooker sensations. I had left him alone to go to the toilet and he must have grabbed the album, chucked it out of the window, where it had landed softly in the flower bed below, in front of our lounge window. I should have known something was up as when I returned, my window was wide open, which it wasn't when I left, and it hadn't been in a long time as it was mid-January and my old man was averse to putting any sort of heating on. Basher seemed edgy all of a sudden, said that he had to go, had to go right now. I thought I had upset him, as I had been beating him on the composite green baize, but that didn't usually bother him. I showed him to the door, returning to the lounge, sat down with mum, and we saw a figure approach the wired glass at the bottom of the window, lean forward, then walk away.

"What's that?" Mum had asked, sounding puzzled.

"I don't know."

"It's very odd, Mike?" She had exclaimed.

I had jumped up, approached the window and seen Basher briskly walking away. At the time I didn't know what he was doing, surely, he had been nicking it, hadn't he?

I still wasn't one hundred percent sure, so I asked Chris Almond. He told me that he had seen my album at Basher's place and not only that, he had been boasting to his mates, that he had nicked Skinner's Crass album and as it was the banned First Sitting; it was probably worth a few quid. I went straight round his after school, he totally denied it, then his sister Carol, who must have heard our raised voices, came in and told him to 'stop being such a wanker and give it back'. Basher listened to his sister, he loved her; she was more of a mum to him than his real mum was, he stopped shouting, calmed down, said he had only borrowed it and left the room to fetch it for me. I nodded a thank you to Carol, who smiled sadly back at me. Basher returned with my album, apologising profusely, like it wasn't his fault, he couldn't help himself, then he offered me half a pouch of old Holborn for my trouble. It was sad to watch, but I knew couldn't trust him, so I stopped seeing him and started looking for a vocalist again.

Dale Colins was a punk from the notorious village, Cold Christmas, which was a few miles away from where I lived, sometimes he used to hang out in the village with a mate of mine, Richard 'Ronnie' O'Keefe. I had talked to Dale Colins about the band on many occasions, he was really interested, telling me that he had started writing lyrics himself. I was impressed, so I asked him what he was writing about, he told me the Police, the Tories and the Monarchy, which sounded good to me, so I asked him if wanted to audition for Virus V1. Dale agreed and asked to just let him know when I was ready. It looked like he might be the one, then a few days later when he was walking up from Cold Christmas to The Village, he had spotted Clare Jonas and me on one of our 'walks out into the countryside', he had followed us around the back of the old church, spying on us, as we got up to some teenage kicks. I didn't know how much he saw, the next day though, when he was up in the village, he told everyone that he had seen me up at the old church with Clare trying to bury a stiffy, which I thought was hilarious, that is, until Clare found out. Clare was absolutely mortified and after that, our 'walks out into the countryside' became a lesson in chastity as she was paranoid that someone could be watching us, she wouldn't even kiss, suddenly I didn't find it so funny anymore.

I was frustrated, furious, so the next time I saw him in the village, making sure that Clare and any other kids who were nearby could hear me, I told him he was a bullshitting wanker, he didn't see anything, to which he had no reply. Dale didn't hang in the village much after that, when I saw him, he would look away, which was sad really; but it seemed to do the trick with Clare as she got back to her normal feisty self, and we went further and further on 'our walks out into the countryside'.

Dale would have been a good vocalist, he was a big bloke with a deep voice, but I didn't want a perv in the band, particularly one with a big mouth, as much as I didn't want a tea-leaf, who steals from me in the band, our search continued.

I saw Richard's younger brother Andy, at his place now and again, although I didn't think of him as mate, as he was a couple of years younger than me, at first glance, he had everything we were looking for in a vocalist. Andy loved punk, particularly the hardcore bands Conflict, Discharge, Crass, the way he dressed reflected that, there were a couple of problems though. One, he was a couple of years younger than us, so we weren't sure if his voice would be aggressive enough for what we needed. Two, and probably more importantly, he was already playing guitar in an established punk band called Necro.

Andy was interested in what we were doing, frequently asking what I was writing, now, and again I would show him some riffs I had been playing around with, he seemed to like what he was hearing. I thought it wouldn't do any harm to audition him, so the next time Richard and me were taking a fag break during one of our many jam sessions, I decided to test the water by asking Richard if he thought Andy would be interested in joining us as a vocalist.

"Yeah, yeah, you should ask him," he said nodding vigorously, blowing out a nimbus cloud of smoke.

A few days later down at Richards, we were working on a new track I had written called 'Christ Fuckers', when Andy not so nonchalantly walked in, plopped himself down on his bed, and after looking at Charlie Harper on the wall for a while, he peered at me expectantly.

"You alright, Andy?" I asked, uncoupling my fingers from the fret board on my guitar.

"Alright Skinner?" He replied, knowing exactly what was coming.

I gave Richard a withering glance.

"Andy, do you fancy singing in our band?"

Andy's face lit up, "Yeah, definitely."

Richard said, "Nice one, OK Andy we'll have two cups of ink tea, with three sugars in each, and if you can find any biscuits, you'll get a Brucie Bonus."

"What's the Brucie Bonus?" Andy laughed.

"You won't have to watch the big, chinned twat on TV tonight, that's a proper bonus," Richard laughed, hitting a couple of bass strings.

Andy laughed too and left for the kitchen, to make the ink.

I smiled, laughing to myself and thought, yeah, I was right, it really is going to be even better being in a band with my mates.

Now it was all coming together; we were a proper four-piece band, we had a name, Virus V1, a couple of tracks, 'Christ Fuckers' and 'Everybody's Boy' with plenty of ideas for more, and most importantly of all, we all had bucket loads of enthusiasm to make it happen. All we needed now was somewhere to practice, and I thought I knew just the place.

Chapter 8

Don't Bullshit a Bullshitter

I suggested to the old man that since my older brother Martin had moved out the year before, I could use his room for Virus V1 band practice, and he suggested I piss off. I wasn't giving up that easily though, so on one of my mum and the old man's rare nights out, I arranged our first practice – my thinking being, that if they came back, found us playing, they might think 'oh it's not so bad' and they'll let us carry on, even if we get a couple of weeks out of it, it would be good just to get us started. Mum had only told me about their 'once in a blue moon' night out the day before, so when I asked Richard to get Andy ready for his first practice Richard apologised, telling me that his family were going out, and they couldn't make it. I couldn't believe it; it was such bad luck, Richard reckoned they hardly ever all went out together either, but I wanted to start practising. I wasn't waiting any longer, so as it turned out, it was only Dave and me at Virus V1's first practice. Dave didn't care, like me, he just wanted to play, so he showed up at my house at five past seven, five minutes after mum and the old man left, and we set up in my brother's cramped, old bedroom.

Virus V1's first practice had only been going ten minutes, when through the wall of sound, we were producing, I heard the front door bang shut and a stampede of feet on the stairs.

In burst the old man, followed closely by my mum.

"What the bloody hell's going on here!?" He shouted.

I flipped the pickups off on my guitar, "We're practising."

"Over my bloody dead body, you are."

Dave holstered his sticks, I put my guitar down, Virus V1's first official practice ended.

"Oh, for goodness' sake, Mike. What's all this? What were you thinking?" My Mum chided, her trust in me wilting a little bit more.

I smiled like butter would melt, "Oh, don't worry, we're just running through a couple of things; we won't turn it up too loud," I said calmly, defusing the situation.

"Bullshit, I could hear you from the top of our road!" The old man snapped.

I laughed, "I doubt it."

"I bloody well could, Michael. That bloody racket will damage the house's foundations, it did when that Rhet friend of yours came over, there was a new crack in the kitchen ceiling!"

I slapped my forehead with my hand, "Oh Jesus, Rhet? His name was Rat," not believing a word of it.

A grin played at the corner of his lips, "Rhet, Rat, Bat, Cat, I don't give a monkey's cuss. Get this junk packed away now, before the whole house comes down."

"Rhet or Rat?" He said, turning to mum, "Frankly my dear, I don't give a damn," bringing a smile to her face.

"I thought you'd like us making some noise, you're always moaning about the bloke across the road using his chainsaw on Sunday mornings, I'm paying him back for you!" I said slyly.

"Oh, yes, nice try, don't bullshit a bullshitter. Now come on, put it away."

I shook my head, resigned, "You worry too much dad"

"Well, some bugger has to," he shot back.

A dismissive look at Dave and a look to the heavens, my old man tramped out of the room, taking a disappointed looking mum with him.

I looked at Dave's amused face, "Sorry mate, it looks like we're going to have to find somewhere else to practice."

One last floor shaking strum of guitar, I switched my amp off, watching the red light fade away.

A couple of weeks went by, still we had nowhere to practice then thankfully, Dave came through for us. Dave loved his football, played for Thundridge FC, who shared a pavilion with the local cricket club, alternating between the football season in the winter and the cricket season in the summer. Dave reckoned the pavilion would be perfect for us, so he asked his old man, Alan, if he could get us in there. Alan was not only popular and well liked in the village, he was also on the board of directors for the football club, so within a few days of Dave asking him, he pulled a few strings, and we were in; we had our place to practice. I was really happy, so the next time I saw Alan, I thanked him for his help. It did have its draw backs, though. On the plus side, the pavilion was about half a mile outside the village, so we could do what we wanted and most importantly make as much noise as we wanted. On the minus side, the pavilion was about half a mile outside the village, and we had no transport, so we would have to hump all of our gear down ourselves. It would be difficult, but in the end, I thought it was a fair trade-off.

On a good day, Virus V1 had three amps, a couple of guitars and Dave's drum kit, so not a great deal of gear, but it is if you have to carry it cross-country. I had a big old-fashioned Laney amp, it was solid, built to last, and with my house being on the opposite side of the village to the pavilion, it was more like a mile away, which is a long way to walk with an amp balanced precariously on your shoulder, especially for me as I did no exercise whatsoever.

Andy and Richard did a bit of boxing, Dave played football most weekends, so they were in good shape, fit and up for the task in front of them, took it all in their stride. I didn't, it was hard going, but I thought there was a bit of pride at stake here, so I humped along with the best of them.

In any weather I would hoist my amp up onto my shoulder, walk down my road, through the white fences next to the vicarage, vault the wall into the churchyard, walk down the shingled hill past the huge cypress trees towards the all-night garage and the promised land of Dave's house where finally with my shoulder burning, screaming for mercy, I would unshoulder my burden, taking a much-needed rest.

Once my gear was at Dave's, if we were lucky, Richard and Andy's old man would have dropped their gear off, then the four of us would shoulder as much as we could, hump the whole lot down to the pavilion, sometimes returning for a second shoulder full. If we weren't lucky and Richard's old man was too busy to help us, or more likely, Richard and me had been jamming at mine during the week, we would have to lug his gear, as well as mine from my house.

One day after practice, I struggled back up my road, red-faced, sweating profusely, to find my old man out the front washing the car.

He smiled maliciously, greeting me with, "Hey Mike, how's the workout going?" Flexing his biceps, chortling to himself.

A couple of times when my amp was embedding itself into my shoulder, I thought about asking him for a lift, I knew what his answer would be though, piss off, and if by some miracle he actually said yes, I didn't think I could trust him in front of my mates, he was bound to come out with something that would make my head implode or my toes curl up.

In the end it was all worth it, as once we had got it all down to the pavilion and set up, we could do exactly what we wanted to do. The first thing we wanted to do was, bang the volume right up, knowing the only person around for miles, was Reg Cooper, the old groundskeeper, steadily pushing the line marker up and down the football pitch in readiness for Saturday's home match.

I was practically interested to see how Andy would get on at our first full band practice, it was his audition after all. I need not have worried, he soon proved that my original reservations were unfounded, as not only did he get the track's diction right, the more he sang, the gruffer his voice got, he certainly sounded aggressive enough for what we needed.

Dave and Richard were solid throughout the whole practice, which I knew they would be, as we had gone through some of our intended tracks months before. In the meantime, they had added their own touches, making them even better, and by the time we had to pack up to let the keenest Thundridge FC football players into their pavilion we had the basics of our first three tracks 'Everybody's Boy', 'Christ Fuckers' and 'Protest', which would be the start of our live set.

I was surprised how well it went musically, not on a personal level though, as Andy and Richard hit it off with Dave straight away, like I thought they would, we were all mates working together, learning how to play in a band, and having a laugh while we were doing it; Virus V1 had had their first practice, the vibe in the band was good, we couldn't wait for the next one.

To save time I went through the nine other tracks I had written for Virus V1's live set with Richard, either at his place or back at mine, which was not only a laugh, it was easy, as Richard's bass playing had, much like Dave's drumming, gone well above my expectations. Andy was easy too, I would either give him my lyric sheets, teach him the chords or lend him one of my homemade Test Tapes, which was the way I used to demo my tracks.

Virus V1 test tapes were like mini albums in sketch form, a quick, easy way to see how our tracks might sound when they were completed. It was a primitive process, to say the least, I used two cassette recorders to over dub the three main elements of the tracks onto one cassette. On one tape I would record the guitar, play the tape back, over dubbing the bass using the other cassette player and then repeat the 'process' with the vocals. On completion, I would give the brand-new test tape, to Andy to listen to, he loved getting a new tape as not only could he hear the diction of the tracks, practice them, get them right, ready for the next practice, he could hear all of the band's new tracks as I wrote them.

Andy never had any problems picking up any of the tracks, as from day one we were on the same wavelength, when it came to vocals and guitar, in fact music in general. Dave was as good as his word, he never stopped practising, loved lashing into his drums and by the time the band was practising regularly, he could play along with both of Rudimentary Peni's E.P.'s, Discharge's 'Why' twelve and The Exploited's 'Punks Not Dead' album, hardly missing a beat.

Dave and me were always looking for opportunities to cut corners or put one over on people so when the football club allowed us to set up on Friday nights, to save time on Saturdays for more practising, Dave had suggested to me that we should have an additional unofficial practice on Fridays to go through what we would be doing the next day, which worked out brilliantly.

A few months of breaking our backs humping gear, practising our tracks constantly, laughing our fucking heads off at everything and anything, soon all of our hard work began to bear fruit; fresh fruit for the rotting vegetables of the music industry, we thought. Virus V1 had twelve solid tracks, we started talking about playing live. We were under no illusions, though, there was still plenty of work to do. If we were going to play live, for us, embarrassment was not an option, we needed to sharpen up, not only as musicians but as a band too. It would follow, if we could improve as a band, then the basic ideas that I had for our tracks would become more sophisticated, free flowing; there was still a long way to go.

The twelve tracks were:

1. Everybody's Boy
2. Christ Fuckers
3. Protest

4. Public Enemy
5. Private War
6. Curfew
7. SSPG
8. No More Genocide
9. Gas Chamber Nursery
10. Suffer Little Children
11. Monarchy
12. V1 Bomb

In amongst the grinding mayhem of our music, our message was…

Fuck the state

If I was born in sin, then I'll die the same

I won't accept your rule of law

You'll die on your knees if you're too scared to stand

I'M THE MENACE TO SOCIETY!?

If you tell me what to do, I'll tell you what you can do

How many white lies will it take to cover up your dark secrets?

Monarchy? Useless shit

You say we live in sin; I say I owe fuck all to your king

Your society, a society built on failure

So many lies, so many lives

Tales of Angelic Upstarts The Cxnterbury Tales

The only shit you give is that you don't give a shit

You can fuck your own Christ

A newborn baby dies inside a tortured soul

Why should we suffer for you?

Fuck your money markets, I'm not buying it

Faith in God will kill mankind.

Chapter Nine

Teardrop

A punk rocker found it hard getting gear outside of London in the early days, so I did what everyone else did; do it yourself. I would take an old jacket, rip the sleeves at the shoulders, then repair it with a variety of safety pins, bulldog clips and chains, adding pin badges to the lapels. It was the same, rip and repair process for the t-shirt. In regard to the trousers, it was handy to have a mum who knew her way around a needle and thread, as you'd need her to drainpipe every pair you had – flairs were for hippies and being a punk, you couldn't trust a hippy. It was D.M.'s or brothel creepers for footwear, then lastly and most importantly the hair. If you had a sister, it was easy; wet your hair, spike it up and nick some of her hair lacquer. I didn't have a sister and my mum's days of doing herself up were long gone, so I used soap, which worked well enough, but it did have its drawbacks.

One hot sunny day, my mates and me were messing around down near the River Rib in the village. It couldn't have been any hotter, so for a laugh I dived in to cool off. A few moments later, feeling revitalised, I resurfaced, and my soaped-up hair had frothed up, turning the surrounding water into a soapy bubble bath. I could hear my mates' raucous laughter from the bank, so I began singing, washing under my arms like I was in the shower and scrubbing away in the grime of the River Rib I thought fucking hell, I really have got to get some proper hair gel.

Once the second wave of punk arrived, it became a whole lot easier, as little adverts started appearing in the back of Sounds for t-shirts, pin badges, jackets and trousers. I spent most of my post office savings, using postal orders buying stuff, and although the t-shirts and some of the jackets were good, the bondage trousers just didn't look right, they looked like they had been made by Dclamare, and nobody wanted to be a Delamare kid, so I never bothered ordering them. I kept on looking though, and eventually I found a Kings Road mail order company called Gringo, and not only did their bondage trousers look good, their prices were affordable too.

I needed a cheque for Gringo as they would not accept postal orders, so I tentatively asked the old man if he could write one out for me, as an advance on my five pounds a week pocket money. I knew what he was like where money was concerned, so I had never bothered asking before and, once I had told him what it was for, worse still where the mail order company was, inevitably, I wished I hadn't as the interrogation began. Who? What? Where? Why? When? Which? How? A whole hour of my short life passed at the speed of a snail making its way down a windowpane, and then finally he passed his verdict – no. It was a rip off.

No wasn't an option, I wanted a re-trial, so I badgered, bothered and harangued him, over the next couple of days, assuring him that I hadn't had any problems with mail order before, and probably, most importantly, from his point of view it would be my money that was at risk.

In the end he relented, with 'OK it's your money' and wrote me out a cheque for ten pounds, which I slipped into an envelope with my order, posted it and sat back, waiting for my brand-new pristine King's Road bondage trousers and Discharge 'fight back' t-shirt to arrive.

A couple of days later, the old man asked me if my gear had come, and I told him sarcastically, no it takes a bit longer than two days, as it normally took about a week. A day later, he asked me the same question, and then the day after that and the day after that. It went on like that for two weeks until, eventually, I realised that, for one reason or another, it wasn't coming. I didn't know if it was a rip off like he'd said, or whether it had been lost in the post. I was dreading telling him. I told him.

"I told you so," he'd said, triumphantly.

It was what he had been waiting for, there were no holds barred now; punk rock was one big rip off, and it was mugs like me that made it easy for criminals to get away with it. I countered that it might have got lost in the post, maybe we should check with the post office, but he wasn't having any of it, he had been ripped off by a bunch of low lives, and that was that, as far as he was concerned. I thought, why did it have to happen when the old man was involved, it's typical, and why was he so pissed off, it was my money. I tried to avoid him over the next few days, as he was turning the whole sad episode into some kind of lesson for life, the lesson being – never trust anyone, never buy anything, never do anything unless you're one hundred percent sure of the outcome, if you're not sure, follow the rules, do what you're told, think yourself lucky.

In the end, like a lot of other punks, I took the pilgrimage up to Kings Road to get my bondage trousers, and just like them, I returned home empty-handed as the prices were astronomical. I couldn't understand it, Levi jeans cost ten pounds, which most people couldn't afford, bondage trousers in Seditionaries cost twenty pounds; punks were mostly from poor backgrounds. It wasn't a totally wasted journey though, as I finally managed to get some decent hair gel, found some magenta hair dye too. It had been great going to Seditionaries (formally Sex), seeing the birthplace of punk, imagining Jones, Matlock, Cook, and Rotten hanging out in there with Vivian Westwood and Malcolm McClaren, still no bondage trousers though.

Paul 'Rat' Collins, our Sods bass playing auditionee or Rhet, as my old man still insisted on calling him, still joking 'frankly he didn't give a damn', if he got his name wrong, asked me if I wanted to buy his Kings Road punk gear, telling me he wasn't into punk anymore. I thought, not into punk anymore? Maybe Rhet might be a better name for you now, mate.

"I don't know, what have you got?" I asked expecting nothing of interest.

"You'll love it, Baker," he said, once again reading me like a book, not a very good one either.

"I've got two cheesecloth Destroy shirts, one with the swastika and the upside-down crucifixion on it, and the other ones the rare God Save The Queen edition with the two pissing cowboys on it, you know the ones with the extra-long sleeves and O-rings like a straitjacket?"

I nodded, "Sounds good Rhet, err… Rat, anything else?"

"I've got a pair of black bondage trousers, if you want them?"

"What from Seditionaries?"

"Yeah, Boy bondage trousers?"

"How much?" I said, way too quickly.

"A fiver will do," he said, putting his hand out to shake on it.

I nearly took his hand off.

Rat presented his bag of punk goodies to me at school the next day, I looked inside, I couldn't have been happier. I gave him the cash and dashed off to the bogs to try my Boy black bondage trousers on, only to discover that Rat's waist was at least two inches smaller than mine.

I struggled slowly rolling them up my legs, inch by inch, I laid down on the bog floor and managed to get them to my waist, the button was two inches away from the hole, I couldn't even do the zip up, it was ridiculous, they looked like I had sprayed the fucking things on, they were so tight.

Downcast, I sold them to Matt Beresford, Bean's younger brother, who couldn't have been happier. Still no bondage trousers.

A few weeks later, a new lead presented itself, unsurprisingly coming from Sounds. In the small ads at the back, I read about a shop in the East End of London called The Last Resort that sold 'Kings Road Punk gear at East End prices,' so me and some of my mates from the village; Danny O'Shea, Lee Walker and his little brother Glyn took the train up to London. I wasn't sure about taking Glyn along with us, as he was four years younger than us, still at primary school, but Lee insisted he wouldn't come without his little brother. Glyn and Lee were so close they came as a pair, so I told Lee that he would have to look out for him, and he said he would.

Once we got into London, we took the tube, alighting at Aldwych East station, and set off on foot into the East End where we found The Last Resort almost straight away. I followed Danny in and saw that once again it was a waste of time. In one corner of the shop, they had a small selection of punk t-shirts, the rest of the shop was packed out with skinhead, rude boy and mod stuff.

Lee and Glyn who were getting into the fast-rising skinhead scene were in their element looking around the rows of Fred Perry shirts, ox blood D.M. boots, braces, pork pie hats, two-tone suits and parkas, I couldn't have been less interested, nor could Danny, so we left them to it, finding a low wall across the road from the shop and sat down.

I pulled out a ready-made roll-up from my bacci pouch, sparked it and sat back watching the East End world go by. It was noisy, colourful, vibrant, it felt like we were sitting at the centre of the world. A couple of roll ups, and a thousand faces later, Lee and Glyn came out of the Last Resort beaming with two pairs of red braces in their hands.

Danny looked at me and rolled his eyes, we dropped off the wall and took a slow wander around Whitechapel, ending up in a pie and mash shop then, after devouring the traditional cockney dish, we returned to the tube station, making our way to the escalators and paced on.

Glyn looked worried as the stairs fell away under his feet.

"You alright, Glyn?" I asked reassuringly.

Glyn nodded back, uncertainly.

"It's OK, don't worry, mate. If you don't want to go down, follow me," I suggested, turning and walking back up the descending escalator.

I was still going down, so using huge lolloping steps I ran against the tide, making my way back up towards the top, my mates cracked up laughing, below me.

A city-type wearing a blue pin-striped suit with matching tie appeared at the top, dodging past me, tutting irritably and carried on down the escalator towards the others, who were now on their way up too, laughing like hyenas as they too ran against the tide.

"Wanker!" I shouted at him.

City-type, zigzagged through my ascending mates and they laughed at his retreating form.

Once I had made it to the top, I strolled over to another escalator that was going down, got on and began to descend all over again. I passed my mates running up the other side and gave them the wankers sign, carrying on down, deeper into the depths of the tube station.

A rush of hot dry air blew into my face, as the next train pushed the air through the tunnel below and up the escalator.

"Oi! Oi, come on! Our train's coming!" I shouted, now running the right way down the stairs.

I ran out onto the platform and pushed the button to open the door, the tube train slowly pulled away, leaving me to watch it disappear, snake like, into the tunnel at the other end of the platform. A moment later, the rest stamped out onto the platform, breathing heavily, their shouts of frustration lost in the breeze of the retreating train, we all cracked up laughing.

"Oh, what! We missed it, you fucking knob-ends," I said, panting like a dog.

Danny took a deep breath and pointed at an automated notice board above us, "It's fine Skinner, look there's another one in two minutes."

"Oh yeah, you alright now Glyn?"

"He's fine," said Lee, putting a protective hand on his little brother's shoulder.

I fumbled in my pocket for my lighter as I watched the train lights vanish into the tunnel.

Out of the corner of my eye, I watched as a gang of about fifteen skinheads appeared on the platform and seeing us, they marched over, surrounding us.

A big skinhead stepped forward at the front of the group, "Oi give us a fag then."

I didn't say anything.

I noticed he had a teardrop tattooed under one of his eyes, eyes which were now scrutinising me like I was a piece of dog shit that he had found on the sole of one of his ox blood D.M.s.

Teardrop snorted and repeated impatiently,
"Come…On…Then…Give…Us… A fag," Gesturing with his hand.

I handed over my roll-up.

"Cheers, I'll save that for later."

Teardrop stuck it behind his left ear and grinned at his mates, before turning back to me, "What about my mates, then? They all smoke, don't you lads?"

The group of skinheads laughed at his audacity.

I looked down, "I haven't got anymore, only one, that's all I got."

"Oh yeah, so if I was to look in your fucking pockets, you wouldn't have nothing then?" He growled suspiciously.

I shook my head. "I've only got one."

It was totally silent on the platform; all I could hear was my heart thumping, heavily in my ears, as the fear took hold.

Teardrop looked around at his gang, grinning again, speaking directly to a skinhead standing next to him in a blue Harrington, he asked, "What do you think, Daz?"

"I don't know, they're just little kids, aren't they? Where do you lot come from?" Daz laughed, shaking his head.

"Err, … We don't come from London." I mumbled nervously.

Teardrop immediately stepped forward, demanded, "Where…Do…You…Come…From?"

"It's north of here," I said, quickly.

"You're not fucking Spurs are yer?"

"I don't like football," I replied, meekly.

Blue Harrington whistled, "You know, that's the best answer you could have given."

The gang laughed, showing their approval.

"Yer, see, we eat Yiddos alive," Teardrop stated. "We hate the Yids, and we hate the Yids," he chanted.

All the skinheads joined in, "WE HATE THE YIDS!"

I felt a gentle breeze touch my face as the next train began its approach to the station, I thought this must be the slowest two minutes of my life. Please hurry up.

"WE HATE THE YIDS AND WE HATE THE YIDS!"

Blue Harrington stepped forward, pushing Danny backwards into Glyn, grinning inanely.

"WE HATE THE YIDS AND WE HATE THE YIDS!"

A tube train shot out of the tunnel, blasting us with its hot dusty air, slowing, hydraulic brakes screeching.

"WE HATE THE YIDS AND WE HATE THE YIDS. WE ARE THE YID HATERS!"

Teardrop leant into me, "You ain't wearing any fucking Rock Against Racism badges, are you?" He asked, examining my pin badges on my lapels, prodding and pulling at them.

"No," I said, thinking that's lucky, my Rock Against Racism badge is on my other jacket.

The tube train came to a creaking halt and the doors hissed open, tantalisingly.

Teardrop examined all of our lapels, then satisfied that no one was wearing any anti-racism badges, he said, "OK, go on then… You can fuck off now."

Blue Harrington pronounced, "Oh you lot, lucky, lucky, lucky, I wouldn't come back to the East End if I was you," stepping aside, so we could get on the train.

Danny, me, Lee and Glyn shuffled, heads down, off the hazardous platform and into the sanctuary of the carriage, where we sat awkwardly, heads still down, cowed, waiting for the doors to close, so this nightmare could be over, then with a single hydraulic hiss. It was.

I watched the blurred image of the skinheads fade through the filthy window as the front of our train entered the tunnel, took a ready-made roll up out of my bacci pouch, sparked it up, took a huge lug, and felt the calming effect of the nicotine spread throughout my shaking body.

"I thought you said you only had one Skinner?" Danny asked, a smile playing at his lips.

"Yeah, one for them. This one's for me," I laughed beginning to compose myself.

"And so are these," I said, opening my full bacci pouch to reveal another ten ready-mades all ready to go, and we creased up laughing at my audacity.

Danny exhaled loudly, "I thought we were going to get a kicking there."

We all nodded our heads in agreement.

I smiled broadly, "Nah, we'd have been fine, Glyn would have sorted them out, wouldn't you Glyn?" Lightening the mood.

"Yeah, you would've, wouldn't you mate?" Lee said, ruffling his little brother's blonde hair.

Glyn smiled at him, looking made up.

Chapter Ten

Rock Against Racism

A couple of weeks after the ill-fated Last Resort trip, my package from Gringo turned up, I didn't know what I was happier about, the triumph of opening it in front of my old man, or the quality of the trousers themselves, they were the highest of standard. Inside the other part of my order, a Discharge Fight Back t-shirt, I found a flyer from People Unite Records informing me of a Rock Against Racism (R.A.R) gig at Brent Park in London with The Ruts headlining. I was even more determined to go after what had happened, so I took the flyer to school and by the end of the day fellow punks; Simon Bamford, Gary Walsh, Matt Beresford (drummer in local punk band Onslaught) and of course Richard, who swore he was never going to miss The Ruts playing again, said they all wanted to go too. I thought with a solid group of punks with me, I will wear my Rock Against Racism badge this time.

People Unite's day of anti-racism was to be my first outdoor festival, in typical British summertime style, the weather was terrible. Brent Park was awash, we were lashed by torrential rain and high winds, the minute we entered the park. In the sky above us, huge sheets of plastic arched chaotically in the wind, having been ripped from the P.A. system in a vain attempt by the roadies to keep it dry. A series of loud thunder cracks from above had us running for shelter under a group of trees at the edge of the park.

"I don't think it's a good idea to be under trees in a thunderstorm," said Richard, sweeping his already soaked spikes back.

Simon flipped some water off his forehead, "No, maybe not"

A huge lightning bolt zigzagged out of the sky, hitting a tower block on the horizon.

"Oh my word!" Said Matt, "We had better move."

"I'm OK, watch this," I said, moving out from the cover of the trees.

I strutted up behind a young couple who were using golf umbrellas to keep the rain off, smoothly slid under the brolly unnoticed and gave my soaked mates the wanker's sign.

A couple of wanker's signs came back at me then my mates disappeared into the group of trees, appearing at the other side, I saw they were heading for the beer tent.

"Er, excuse me mate, but what are doing?" An irritated voice said.

I turned, seeing two pissed off faces, "Er sorry I'm… Err looking for the beer tent, it's over there yeah?" I said, breaking cover.

Dodging clusters of soaking people and huge mirror like puddles, reflecting the gun metal sky above, I finally caught up with my mates as they queued up outside the beer tent. Once we had been served our five pints of snakebite, we huddled up close to the beer tent in a futile attempt to keep some of the rain off; it was hardly worth it. I took a swig of my drink, nodding appreciatively in our collective huddle. As the amber liquid hit the spot, I heard the sound of raucous chanting. Gary heard it too, his eyes squinting up tightly to keep the piecing rain at bay, he looked to the front area, near the stage.

"Oh, fucking hell," he said.

I followed his gaze through the blitzkrieg of pouring water, I couldn't believe my now stinging eyes- there must have been about a hundred skinheads.

Richard asked, "Are they who I think they are?"

"Yeah, wankers, let's go and have a look at some wankers," said Gary, a malicious smile playing at the corner of his mouth.

Simon nodded as we stalked out of our pitiful shelter, immediately being hit by sheets of rain.

Gary marched on ahead, Simon at his shoulder, the rest of us following. Before us the whole sunken park opened up, the bending tents, a sodden stage, labyrinths of winding plastic, millions of pieces of paper thrown up in mini tornados and in amongst it all, the skinheads stood.

I could see them a lot more clearly now we were closer, some of them were pissing in bottles, chucking them over their shoulders into a group of about twenty punks, who we had just joined, some of the punks were chucking them back.

"WE HATE THE YIDS AND WE HATE THE YIDS, WE HATE THE YIDS AND WE HATE THE YIDS AND WE HATE THE YIDS, WE ARE YID HATERS!"

A couple of ice-cold fingers scratched down my spine as the memory of a teardrop under a drunken, bloodshot eye forced its way to the surface of my mind. In the tube station, helpless, heart pumping, scared out of our wits, waiting, relying on a train to come to our rescue, we could do nothing, you were right we were just kids, four kids against at least fifteen of you. It's another day now, though. I felt anger, anger at their culture, clothes, music, at their stupid, tribe-like obsession with the complete waste of time that is football.

I picked up a plastic bottle of inky yellow liquid off the ground and hurled it at the mass of bald heads, watching it rise, spinning through the baying winds, spraying its piss cargo all over them and finally crashing down, in amongst them.

A cheer rose up behind me, I turned to find Gary beaming at me, his hands full of bottles ready to launch his own aerial assault, it was now a total free for all, everybody was at it, grabbing the plastic bottles, topping them up, hurling them, laughing, enjoying the stupidity of it all.

"It really is pissing down," Richard said, laughing.

Richard was right, too; the air was quite literally full of piss.

"Piss off Skinheads," I shouted back at Richard, launching another bottle into the blasting wind.

The Skinheads didn't like a taste of their own medicine, they lobbed some glass bottles back in our direction, they came hurtling towards us, so we ducked for cover, that was it, the game was over. I slowly got up off my haunches, mouth agape, shaking my head in their direction.

"What a bunch of cunts," Gary stated abruptly, still standing upright.

I watched the security guards rush over to the glass throwers, remonstrating with them and soon, skinheads nearby saw what was happening to their mates, coming to their aid, surrounding the security, pushing, shoving, shouting at them. A few of them stood their ground, standing strong, pushing back, they didn't hold out long though, there were just too many skinheads, and they were being overrun. It was getting out of control, it was dangerous, escalating fast, it was time to get out of there, time to retreat.

Inside the sanctuary of the stage area, a watching group of roadies saw the danger too, steeling themselves, they ventured out coming to the aid of the stranded security guards. One took a vicious right hook to the face, spinning him helplessly, before he fell backwards into the piss soaked mud. A couple of skinheads broke away from the main pack, smelling wounded prey, and stuck the boot in, viciously kicking the roadie, while he floundered on the ground pathetically, shouting for help. A combination of the rest of the roadies and the retreating security guards eventually pushed the rampaging boot boys aside, pulling the helpless bloke up, hauling him off towards the safety of the backstage area, and once inside they locked the high metal gates behind them.

A massive cheer went up, it was another victory, fists punched into the air, the chanting of the skinheads got louder, louder, louder and as the chanting intensified, the weather intensified, and the seconds of the afternoon ticked away before us.

"You know what. I think it's going to be called off," I sighed.

"Oh, fucking hell. I'm going to miss them, again, aren't I?" Richard despaired.

Right on cue, there was a shriek of feedback from the stage, and someone from RAR appeared, bravely stepping out onto the sodden bottle strewn stage. He apologised for the delay, stating that because of the weather, they were having some technical problems, and thank you for your patience. No one could touch the skinheads now, and they knew it, so they rained more bottles down onto the stage, and he exited stage left as fast as his legs could carry him.

Gary said, "Bastards, come on, let's give them some back," hurling bottles back at them.

Matt dropped down onto his haunches, snatched up a half-full of something plastic bottle, launching it high into the chaos above us. It flew up into the metal grey sky, where it got caught by a gust, blowing it back onto a group of punks standing in front of us.

"Oi, which one of you stupid wankers chucked that?"

I turned around to make it look like the bottle had been thrown by someone behind us, and as my eyes began to focus, from out of the watery haze came a large group of punks.

I thought, crazily, the cavalry are here, we are saved.

It wasn't the cavalry though; it was Dave Ruffy and Mannah followed by the rest of the band.

"Oh what, look, it's the Ruts," I said.

"It is as well," responded Simon.

Matt who was being dossed out by a big angry looking punk with stale beer or something worse in his Mohican said, "Yeah it is, come on!" Keen to get away.

Matt rushed up to greet them, the rest of us following close behind him.

I walked confidently up to Dave Ruffy.

"Alright Dave?" I asked, like I was greeting an old mate.

Dave Ruffy ran a hand through his thinning hair, looking curiously at me.

"Yeah, good, cheers."

"You remember me from the moonlight club? I got there really early?" I asked.

"Yeah, we played the moonlight club."

Dave Ruffy didn't have a clue who I was, and I thought, why would he? He must have done a hundred gigs and met a thousand people since then.

I recovered myself, "Yeah, that was a good gig that. I saw you at the Lyceum too."

Dave Ruffy nodded, "Cheers, we like playing the Lyceum." Grinning at a memory.

John Fox, the guitarist, leant in between us, "What are you talking to these kids for?" He said dismissively.

"Nah, it's fine they're into us, they're OK," Dave Ruffy replied.

John Fox took a puff on his fag and shrugged his shoulders, turning to Malcolm Owen, with an amused look on his face.

I hadn't seen Malcolm Owen close up since the moonlight club gig, a year or so earlier, he didn't look well at all, his bony arms poked out of his ostentatious Hawaiian shirt like sticks, his face glistened with sweat. He seemed jittery too, continuously bouncing from foot to foot, all the while sweeping his lank black fringe back from the gaunt, stretched skin on his forehead.

Segs the bass player joined us, "I think the gig's off," he stated, ducking as a hail of plastic bottles rained down on us, grinning madly.

"What a bunch of wankers, eh?" Gary said.

"Yeah… Well it's not all of them, I know plenty of cool skinheads… And rude boys, they're some good people," Dave responded.

I nodded doubtfully, "Yeah, really?"

"Yeah, we've got a new song about them, it's called 'Staring at the Rude Boys'," he informed us.

"I'd like to do more than that to the bastards," Gary stated, staring at the rude boys.

Dave laughed at the kid's bravado, "No, it's nothing like that. It's a song of unity, we want to unite people."

On that positive note, he left us to mingle with some of the other punks who had come over, to talk to the band.

"Oh, well you got to see The Ruts after all, Rich," I said turning to my distraught looking mate.

Richard gave me a withering look and grabbed a bottle, "I'm going to miss them again, aren't I… Fuck this!" he shouted, lobbing it with all of his might.

It spun over the crowd and scored a direct hit on a bald pate.

Richard cackled at me, giving me a thumbs up, feeling a bit better now.

Another bloke from RAR hesitantly came on stage and made the final announcement, the announcement we all knew was coming.

"I'm really sorry but due to the bad weather conditions, we are not going to be able to go ahead with this afternoon's entertainment," he said, as another volley of bottles rained onto the stage. "I'm so sorry, and so are the organisers. Please have a safe journey home and remember… We are stronger, together, all of us… Black and white unite…People unite and fight racism…"

Inevitably the skinheads cheered another victory, launching another massive barrage of bottles, peppering his running figure until he was off the stage. It was the skinhead's cue for a full invasion, they rampaged forward, ramming the depleted security out of the way, pouring onto the stage, and they then turned in unison, to face the audience at the Rock Against Racism gig, raising their right arms in the air, shouting…

"SIEG HEIL, SIEG HEIL, SIEG HEIL, SIEG HEIL, SIEG HEIL, SIEG HEIL!"

"SIEG HEIL, SIEG HEIL, SIEG HEIL, SIEG HEIL, SIEG HEIL, SIEG HEIL!"

Gary spat, "Yeah, sure, some of them are alright, what a bunch of bastards," picking up a glass bottle, drawing his arm back.

Simon grabbed his arm, "Nah, don't do it Gary, don't lower yourself to their level."

Gary knew right from wrong deep down, even if his temper didn't. The bottle dropped back into the mire with a clink.

"I don't get it, it doesn't make sense, how can skinheads spend the day hating black people and then spend the whole night dancing to music made by black people, what a bunch of cunts," I concluded, staring at the stage of bald heads pumping their right arms in the air.

"SIEG HEIL, SIEG HEIL, SIEG HEIL, SIEG HEIL, SIEG HEIL, SIEG HEIL!"

Richard rubbed at his face, "I wondered that myself"

"SIEG HEIL, SIEG HEIL, SIEG HEIL, SIEG HEIL, SIEG HEIL, SIEG HEIL!"

Brent Park stood in silence, watching the skinheads pay homage to the Fuehrer, grinning like they had won some great victory, I thought, you idiots wouldn't have lasted two minutes in the Third Reich, you would have gone up the chimney with all the other 'undesirables'.

I shook my head slowly, "I'm not standing here, watching this, let's get out of here."

Simon, took a glance at Gary who was now snarling, seething with anger and put a placating hand on his shoulder. "Yeah, I think we better… Come on Gary, you don't need any more trouble in your life right now, mate."

Gary nodded slowly, accepting the situation, using his brain again.

"OK, I think it's this way, come on," I suggested.

Richard, Matt, Gary, Simon and me left the baying Nazis to their 'great victory', trudging back laboriously through the howling wind and sheets of rain to Neasden tube station, feeling broken, defeated and confused about the world we lived in.

Chapter Eleven

A Dedicated Follower of Fashion

London was full of skinheads, Madness, The Specials, Bad Manners, and The Selector were now playing regularly to the mass of bald heads in the capital, and with the kind of exposure they were getting, they soon began to dominate the mainstream charts, meaning the movement seeped out of London into the suburbs, into my village. Skinhead culture was everywhere, popular music was changing, and again young people were changing with it, most of my mates were either buying two-tone suits, pork pie hats or Fred Perry shirts to wear with their ox blood D.M. boots and braces. The skinhead movement was a complete waste of time, as far as I was concerned, it had come and gone in the 1960s, so what was the point of bringing it back now, then I thought about the money my mates must be spending, and I had my answer. It wasn't just my mates in the village that were changing, going skinhead, rude boy. Richard was changing too, gone were the punk t-shirts, black drainpipes, it was all Fred Perry's and Levi stay pressed now, as for his trademark blonde Billy Idol spikes, they were scalped off to make way for a number one.

Billy Idol had metamorphosed into Terry Hall in under a month and when I asked him about it, he said, 'I guess I'm just a dedicated follower of fashion,' which just made his conversion even worse, as punk was never a fashion to me, it was a way of life.

It was a worrying development, I thought, it didn't necessarily have to be a problem with Virus V1 though, there were a lot of bands like The Angelic Upstarts, Sham 69 and The Cockney Rejects around, who were skinheads inspired by the Sex Pistols to play punk rock. A lot of skinheads were into punk too following The Clash, The Exploited and the Anti Nowhere League. In the end I reasoned that

Richard was not only our bass player, an important part of the band, he was also a good mate, who got on with everybody, so apart from the band chanting the odd, "Skinheads! Skinheads!" Or "Foreskin heads!" When he walked into practice with his pate shining in the early morning sunshine, nothing really changed, to start with.

Richard had been given the route notes to all of our tracks when we had first got together. In the following months, between jamming with me and working on his own, he had come up with some pounding rock basslines, which sat perfectly in the middle of my industrial guitar riffs and Dave's rampaging drums, but as Richard got more into Ska, the original skinhead's music, he began to shoehorn Ska bass licks into our music. This not only made a mockery of what we were trying to do, it sounded comical, satirical, like we were taking the piss out of ourselves. I hated 'On my radio' by The Selector, it was one of the most vacuous pieces of shit I had ever heard, particularly the way the bass walks up the frets at the end of each bar.

Doom, dee, doom, dee, Doom

I had heard that bassline a million times before quite literally, on my radio, mainly on disco tracks, during the Cosmic's phase. It really is the same old show on your radio, because of the shite that you are producing, I thought.

One day, we were surging through 'Christ Fuckers', shaking the pavilion to its foundations when… Doom dee doom dee doom dee whimpered out of Richard's bass amp. I stopped playing, Dave dropped his sticks, Andy pretended to chuck his mic through the window, and we all fell about laughing, wondering what the fucking hell we had just heard.

"What the bloody hell was that... Jesus," Dave asked, slapping his head theatrically.

"I haven't got a clue," I said mystified at first, "Oh no, hold on, is it 'Christ fuckers on my Radio'?"

"It's just the same old show," Andy crooned back at me, laughing.

Dave and me creased up laughing, both eyeing our bass player, wondering what he was up to.

"I just thought I'd give it a try," Richard said, innocently.

"You can fuck your own The Selector," Andy sang to his brother.

Andy, Richard, Dave and me got back to it, flew through the rest of 'Christ Fuckers' and 'Protest', then when we came to the chorus of 'Public Enemy', it was the same old show.

Doom dee, doom dee, Doom flounced out of his amp, we stopped creasing up laughing.

I sighed inwardly, thinking of all the Ska tracks, why does it have to be that one, if it had been 'A Night Boat to Cairo' riff or even a 'Baggy Trousers' one, I might have let it go but 'On my Radio' by The Shit-lector – no chance. It was too much. It was to get much worse.

On 'Private War', He Heaven 17-ed.

Dee Doom Dee Doom Dee...

'Monarchy', he A.B.C-ed

Dee Doom, Dee Doom, Bap, Bap…

'Suffer Little Children' was OK until the slow part at the end when Andy reads out parts of Deuteronomy from the bible.

Doom, Dee, Doom, Dee, Doom… He Duran Duran-ed.

It couldn't carry on, it was Carry-On, our Sid Vicious was metamorphosing into Sid James, Dave, Andy and me came to a stuttering halt.

In the last verse of 'V1 Bomb' he Soft Cell-ed.

Dee, Dee, Dee, Dee, Dee, Dee, Doom, Doom…

Once again, we came to a juddering halt, Dave slapped his head again, only this time with a lot more force, beginning to lose his patience, none of us were laughing now.

I sighed inwardly, thinking enough is enough, "Oh, come on Rich, we can't have that mate," I said, seriously.

Richard sniggered mischievously, nodding his head, "OK, Skin" he said sticking his thumb up.

I smiled back at him knowingly.

A few tracks later…

Doom Dee, doom Dee, Doooom… Simpered out of his amp.

I was expecting it this time, so instead of stopping, I gave him a patient look, like you would give a particularly annoying child, and got back to my guitar. Not only was it annoying, it distracted the band away from what I thought we should have been doing, tightening up, improving, getting ready to play live. I thought Richard was being petulant, like he was trying to show his little brother that he could play what he wanted to, and he could if it was punk rock. Dave was playing punk rock; I was playing punk rock and Andy was punk through and through, so there was no place in the band for any kind of Level 17 slap bass nonsense.

Richard and me had been mates for a long time, though, been through plenty, had some great laughs, we were always taking the piss out of each other, never took anything to heart, so even though this was frustrating in the extreme, I hoped that this was just another part of it.

A couple of days after Doom dee, doom dee, doom and subsequent bass crimes, had reared their ugly heads at our practice, Richard told me he wanted to play other types of music, as well as punk. I thought, OK yeah, I'm up for that too, try something new, any excuse to play my guitar and maybe, just maybe, if we played something different, he might get the shit music out of his system, be more likely to play our Virus V1 tracks as we had first envisaged them.

Once we had finished our next Saturday's practice, lugged our gear up to mine and got a bite to eat, we settled down to try something new, something Richard liked. Richard slapped out a funky bass line, grinning and baring it, I picked up my guitar. In keeping with trying something different I challenged myself to avoid using bar E or bar A, although, it was tough going to start with, bloody tough going, I loved bar E, I got into it, floating notes, harmonics, making up chords, which served as melodies. I was surprised, I liked what I was hearing, it was cold, it was rhythmic, it was like nothing I had ever heard before, sitting somewhere in between the beats of Theatre of Hate and the grind of Killing Joke.

A few weeks after our experimentation began, thankfully, the shit that was 'On my Radio' stopped rearing its ugly head at our practices. It seemed to have done the trick, it was business as usual, we went back to doing what we were supposed to be doing, polishing up our sound, tightening up our playing and by doing so, improving as a band. I felt like we were all going in the same direction again, with Richard back playing his solid punk rock riffs. In fact, he was playing better than ever, and because of that, it lifted us all, we fed off our re-born punk bass player.

I started thinking that it might be a good thing having a skinhead in the band after all, as we had more chance of changing the skinhead point of view with one of their number in the band, also if we were playing live and a horde of them showed up, maybe we wouldn't get bottled off either.
Skinhead or no skinhead in the band, the fact was, it was time to start looking for gigs, we really wanted to play live in front of people, get ourselves out there, see how we went down and if the reception was bad, so what, first and foremost our band was for us. Andy had plenty of mates around Hertford, Ware and Hoddesdon, as did I, so we kept our ears open for anything.

A Saturday morning spent at the pavilion practising should be a laugh, everyone talking, getting on and working together, at our next practice though, Richard wasn't his usual self. He became quieter and quieter as the morning went on, withdrawing from the rest of us, playing like he was just going through the motions, even Andy, his brother, looked confused with his behaviour. I didn't know what his problem was, I couldn't work it out, I had never seen him so quiet before, in fact I had never seen him quiet ever, he always seemed to have plenty to say.

I wanted to ask him what it was then and there, it could have been embarrassing asking him in front of the others though, especially if it was something personal, so I thought I would leave it until later, maybe by then he might have worked it out for himself.

Once we had finished for the day, Richard and me made our way back up to mine, for our usual post-practice afternoon jam session. He still wasn't saying much, if he had a problem, I thought, it's up to him to broach the subject whatever it is, so after a bite to eat, we went up to my bedroom and I made ready for an afternoon of 'Theatre of Joke' as we named our new music.

Richard sat down on my bed, looking at me solemnly, "Skin, I don't want to be in the band anymore mate."

I was absolutely stunned; I wasn't expecting that, "What? No mate. Why?"

"I'm just not into it anymore. It's not my kind of music anymore, Skin."

I sighed deeply, I felt like I'd been blindsided, my eyes welled up with tears, "Oh no, no mate, Jesus, no, no," I said shaking my head.

"Sorry Skin," he responded.

I thought, oh what, after all these months? Fucking hell, we were ready to gig. You can't go now, we're mates, you don't do that to a mate. Do you?

"I'm sorry Skin, I'm just not into it anymore, it's not my thing now."

"Yeah, I suppose so, but… Nah mate, come on," I said looking at him, helplessly.

Richard slumped forward, shaking his head slowly from side to side, "I'm not into it anymore, you can see that, can't you Skin? We both know it, it's not my thing."

I could see he was enjoying telling me, as much as I was enjoying hearing it.

I snorted and laughed, hollowly, "I had noticed," I said, resigning to it, if he wanted to leave, he wanted to leave, what am I going to say, no? Beg him to stay? Nah, definitely not.

"I promise you Skin, it's not going to a problem, I've found you another bass player. Andy knows him, he's into punk… Into punk in a big way and really wants to play in the band," he said, brightening up.

"OK mate, sounds good mate, listen it's fine, if you're not into it, you're not into it, it's just the way it is," I said, beginning to compose myself.

I picked up my guitar, grinning at him, and played.

Doom dee doom dee Doooom…

Richard cracked up laughing and patted me on the shoulder, "It's going to be fine mate; you'll see, we'll still be mates and that. I'll still see you around at school."

"Yeah, yeah, yeah, definitely, I'll still see you at school," I said hopefully.

"I've got to go now," he said, rising quickly.

"OK mate, I'll see you out," I said, making my way slowly to the door.

I thought about it when I got into bed that night, and the more I thought, the more upset I got. I couldn't believe it, was it the end for Virus V1? The end, before we had really got started? What about all of the work we had done, all of the time we had spent on our music, all the time we had spent lugging the amps down to the pavilion, was it all for nothing?

I felt sick, betrayed, angry, confused, my whole idea of being in a band with my mates was that I had people around me that I could trust, so if there was a problem, then as mates we could sort it out together, that just hadn't happened, maybe, it wasn't just about the band, there might be more to it.

Richard had been more studious in the few classes that we shared together at school, I wasn't sure what that was all about, but I couldn't see why that should affect anything. One thing I did know was, he wasn't into punk rock anymore, so it was up to me to accept that, move on, it was the only way. On the plus side, he had been good enough to get us a replacement, which showed he was still a good mate, so I reasoned that it was just one of those things, one of those things that happens, one of those things that happened to me this time.

I told myself, it's not the end, no way, it's time to think about a new beginning.

Virus V1 will continue, keep practising, improving, get better and yes, we will play gigs, just not as soon as I had expected. I stretched out, drifted off to sleep wondering what our new bass player would be like, and if he plays…

Doom dee doom dee doom…

I'm going to ram his bass guitar up his fucking arsehole.

Chapter Twelve

Judy is a What?

Into our next practice walks Paul Hammersmith, a mountain of a kid, dressed in a white, Black Flag t-shirt, black drainpipe trousers and huge black spikes sticking up on top of his head. In one of his shovel-like hands, he carried a compact bass amp, in the other, a classic Sid Vicious bass guitar, white with the black scratch plate. I thought so far so good. Andy introduced us and I showed Whiff, as he liked to be called, the route notes to the first three tracks of our set, 'Everybody's Boy', 'Christ Fuckers', 'Protest' and we got straight down to it, business-like.

Whiff was using a plectrum, which I wasn't into for bass guitar, so at the end of 'Everybody's Boy', I asked him if he could play bass using his fingers instead. I told him, I thought bass guitar should be part of the rhythm section, not just like another rhythm guitar riding over the top of it. It was a separate instrument, it needed to bounce. A lot of punk bass players used a plectrum and the rhythm of the tracks seemed to get lost in the guitar, if Whiff used his fingers instead, finger picking, it would make it easier for him to mould his bass lines around the drums, particularly the bump of the bass drum, and that in turn would give us a solid bridge between the guitar and Dave's drums.

Whiff told me, "No problem, I can play with both," and that was the end of our bass problems.

New-look Virus V1 went over the first three tracks for the rest of the practice, and by the end of the day it was clear for all to see that Whiff was a good enough bass player for what we needed. A few weeks of solid practising went by, Whiff learnt our entire set, putting in his own touches, bringing his style of playing to the band, building the bridge between bass guitar and drums. Once again, we were under way, heading in the right direction, we weren't at the same standard as we were before though, which was to be expected but what Dave and me didn't expect was how much the vibe in the band would change after bringing someone new in.

Whiff was a quiet, unassuming type of kid, who for some reason seemed to be a bit wary of Dave and me, I didn't know why, I had a bit of an undeserved reputation, but Dave didn't. Whiff took some of the things we said way too seriously, and again I didn't know why, as it was obvious to us that we didn't take life too seriously. Dave and me just presumed he didn't have the same sense of humour as the rest of us.

Once we started talking music though, punk in particular, that was it, he would open up, laugh, make jokes himself and any reservations he had about us vanished. Whiff and me would natter away for ages about who was good, who was shit, puffing away on our roll ups, until either Andy or Dave told us, in frustrated tones, that we should stop gassing and get back to practising. One thing that became apparent about Whiff very early on, was that not only did he understand our music and punk in general, he was also conscious of the world around us and the sort of shit going on for so many people, so he understood our message too.

In fact, sense of humour aside, Whiff was Virus V1, through and through, so when he invited me around to his house in Ware for a Sunday afternoon jam, even though I still didn't really know him all that well, I was more than happy to accept.

Whiff lived in Ware, not too far from Andy, so I took the all too familiar two-mile walk down the A10, getting to his house in Milton

Road by the early afternoon. I knocked the blue door, and it opened immediately to reveal a black-haired woman in her late sixties, a pair of thick milk-bottle glasses perched on her nose.

A huge welcoming smile creased up her face, "Oh hello, you must be Mick? Paul! Paul! Mick's here!" She shouted behind her, ushering me inside.

"I'm Paul's mum. You can call me Judy."

"Oh hello, OK thanks," I replied.

"Paul, Paul, Paul! Where are you? Oh dear," She called upstairs, receiving no response. "Oh my, where is he?"

"Oh dear, did you walk down, Mick?" She continued.

"Yes Mrs. Hammersmith, er... Judy"

"Paul, Paul, Paul, PAUL!!"

"Can I get you a cup of tea Mick?"

Whiff appeared at the top of the stairs, put his hand up, greeting me and marched down, rolling his eyes at his fussing mum.

"Oh Paul, there you are, oh dear." Judy repeated, "I'll make some tea, shall I?" Brightly.

Whiff sighed impatiently, "I'll do it. I'll do it. I'll do it!" He said, testily, hoping to end their conversation.

Judy scrutinized him through thick glass lenses, for a moment, despairing at her son, finally shaking her head,

"Oh, Paul!" She despaired some more, retreating into the front room.

"Fucking old slag," Whiff responded, before the door shut behind her.

I did a double-take and half-smiled at him, he burst out laughing.

Oh what, I thought, did I hear that right, did he really just say 'fucking old slag' to his mum? Nah, surely not.

"You alright Skinner? Come in here, mate," said Whiff, walking into the kitchen, pulling me away from my confusion – nah, no way he couldn't have said that.

Whiff made two cups of tea, we took a sip each, to stop it spilling over the edges and carefully made our way upstairs to his bedroom, the box room at the back of the house.

Whiff opened the door, entered, I couldn't believe my eyes.

A huge Technics Sound System towered high in one corner of the room, at its side sat two ominous speakers, on the walls above and around them, posters of punk bands adorned every wall and in amongst this shrine to punk rock there were albums, hundreds of albums. On his bedside table blocking out the light from the window, piled up on the floor in hazardous stacks, on cupboards, shelves and even on his bed. Whiff shifted a couple of albums aside and sat down on his bed. I moved a few more, joining him. While we slurped our tea, he proceeded to tell me that he was getting into the

American hardcore punk scene, listing about twenty bands I had never heard of. Once he had finished his punk mini-tour of America, stopping off at something new called Skate Punk, he asked me if was into any of the American punk bands.

"The Dead Kennedy's are OK," I said, suddenly feeling like I knew nothing about Punk.

Whiff nodded confidently, grabbing, 'Fresh Fruit for Rotting Vegetables' from one of the teetering towers and cued it up.

'California Über Alles' was brilliant, and I was thinking about buying 'Fresh Fruit' and then I heard 'Kill the Poor' and 'Holiday in Cambodia', which I thought were shit, so I didn't bother with it. I was soon nodding my head along with Whiff though, the album was brilliant, it was a real surprise, full of gems, like 'Let's Lynch the Landlord' 'Ill in the Head' and we both creased up at the twisted hilarity of 'Stealing People's Mail'

"Can I borrow this?" I asked, hopefully.

"Yeah of course you can, mate."

Whiff laughed as the opening bars of 'Viva Las Vegas' rang out.

"Oh, no, not this, it's just for a laugh this one, they do a version of 'Rawhide' too, you know that old western program? Clint Eastwood's in it."

"Nah, mate," I shook my head, still not knowing much.

Whiff snatched the needle up, saving us from the Elvis Presley cover, flipped the album over in his hands, slid it safely back into its cover and his bedroom door cracked open.

Whiff sighed expansively.

Judy entered the bedroom, beaming at me, "Oh, sorry, have you finished with the teacups, Paul?"

"YES…" He replied, irritably.

"Oh, Paul," she declared. "I'll just get them now, shall I?"

"If you have to."

Judy removed our cups from the bedside table, revealing two white rings. She looked at Whiff accusingly, "Oh, Paul, you've made a muck here, haven't you? I'll have to get a cloth now."

"It's fine, it's fine. I'll do it in a minute," Whiff said abruptly, eyes flashing a warning.

"Oh, Paul," she admonished.

Whiff's mum gawked at me with a semi amused 'what can I do?' face, while she collected our cups up, putting them on a tray.

"Oh, Paul," Judy chided, walking to the door.

Whiff sniffed loudly, "Stupid fucking old slag."

Judy paused, it looked like she was going to turn around and say something, then she thought better of it, gently shutting the door behind her and her footsteps plodded down the stairs.

"Why do you do that, man?" I asked.

Whiff smirked, "Oh, she's alright. She doesn't worry about it."

"You reckon?" I snorted, not believing a word of it.

Whiff thought about it for a moment and let out a hesitant little laugh, shrugging his shoulders.

"OK mate, do you want to jam then?" I asked.

Whiff nodded his head enthusiastically, "Skinner, there are a couple of tracks I'm not sure of, can we go through them first?"

"Yeah, of course mate."

I unzipped my guitar case, pulled out my Hondo, asking him what tracks he wasn't sure of, while I plugged it into his amp, and we got straight to work.

Whiff and me practised Virus V1 tracks for a couple of hours or so, then as evening came on, and the light faded outside his bedroom window, we decided to call it a day.

I had plans for the evening, I was meeting up with some of my mates in the village, for our annual Halloween trip up to The Old Church, a very famous and some said haunted church just outside the village, I had to get moving. While we were packing up, we discovered that we had another thing in common: an interest in motorbikes. Whiff had always wanted one as a kid, so had I, and we blathered away, talking Yams, Suzi's and Kwaks, for another half an hour, ending up on his doorstep.

Whiff said he was interested in getting something small to start with, maybe a moped.

"If it's a scooter, you'll have to leave the band, I fucking hate scooters," I joked. "And the wankers who ride them," I added.

Whiff protested, "No, no, it's nothing like that. It's just a moped."

"Nah, you're fine. I'm probably going to wait until I can get a proper bike. I'm not really into mopeds… Look seriously, I've got to go man."

"Yeah, yeah. Of course, mate."

I went to leave, and the lounge door cracked open.

Whiff looked around, letting out the longest of sighs, knowing what was coming.

"Ooh, are you going now, Mick?" She asked.

I smiled, "Yes, Mrs. Hammersmith. Thanks for the tea."

"OK, that's fine. I'll see you again soon. Bye Mick."

A small black dog ran out of the lounge, yapping a warning at the stranger on his doorstep.

"MICK! MICK! MICK!" Judy called out, he wasn't having any of it, though, this stranger was still on his territory, he wasn't running away.

"NO MICK, NO, NO MICK!" Judy persisted, "MICK, MICK, NAUGHTY, MICK... Oh..."

Judy stopped in her tracks. Suddenly embarrassed, she shrieked with laughter, "I'm sorry Mick. Mick's the name of our dog!" Said Judy, catching the unruly canine Mick by his collar, leading him back towards the open lounge door.

Whiff looked at me, "What a stupid fucking old slag," he concluded.

Mick let out one final warning yap and the door slammed shut.

I said, "Whiff Jesus mate, that's a little bit harsh, isn't it?"

Whiff looked at me blankly. I thought, why would he know the return comment, it's an in joke, he hardly knows me, come on let's get out of here.

"OK, mate, right. Look I'll see you next week at practice," I said, before turning and walking away, shaking my head sadly.

Chapter Thirteen

Cold Christmas

I was looking forward to seeing my mates, we were going up to the old church or St Mary's and All Saint's Church, to give it it's proper name. It was a couple of miles east of the village and was renamed Cold Christmas Church after rumours circulated that the graveyard was full of children who died in the nearby hamlet of Cold Christmas, after a particularly severe winter. It was built after the Norman conquest in 1086 and then scavenged to build the new church in the middle of the village around two-hundred years later, as the settlement grew.

A lot of superstition surrounded the original structure, which for some reason was built north to south rather than east to west like the traditional Norman churches. In the years since it had been built, there had been sightings of ghosts and many macabre tales told. I was local. I knew the place, had been up there a thousand times, even when I was a little kid, I didn't believe a word of it. For my mates and me, it was just another place to piss about in and sometimes, if we were lucky, we would find people up there and scare the shit out of them.

Mark Worby, Sid Crane, Kevin Green, Dave 'Trotsky' Fitzwalter and me, all final year inmates of Thundridge JMI school or Thundridge Junior Mental Institution as we called it, would break into the main tower regularly. It was simple to say the least, we would rip one of the boards off a lower window then lift each other up onto our shoulders, so we could reach up to the window frame. Once you had grabbed the window frame, if you had the strength, you could haul yourself up, in through the window, then lower yourself down the ten-foot drop to the floor.

Inside, the tower was almost pitch black, the only light coming from the windows at the top of the tower, shining down on you like two biblical spotlights. A few of us braver ones would then walk, arms outstretched to the spiral staircase on the opposite side of the tower, enter it, then bending double we would carefully trek around and around to the top. You had to be careful as you approached the top of the spiral staircase, as the belfry floor had rotted away. One step too many and your foot would land on nothing but air, and you would find yourself falling the thirty feet to the bottom of the tower.

A series of beams running around the tower were all that remained of the floor, once me and my mates were in the belfry, we would dare each other to walk around the tower on them or 'walk the boards' as we christened it. It was fraught with danger as the rotting beams were so narrow, you had to lean tight into the tower's wall, using a slow tandem gait. If that wasn't bad enough, some of the beams were loose, which meant that when you tentatively placed your foot down, they would dip under you, creaking ominously; worse still, if you lost your nerve, you were in big, big, trouble as once you had started, with the beams being so narrow, it was impossible to turn around, so you would have to continue and traverse the entire tower, no matter how scared you were or how much your legs shook. It never stopped us, though.

One night I had boasted to my mum about 'walking the boards' and she went absolutely mental, making me swear never to do it again, so I swore I wouldn't, and I meant it. I told my mates that I had sworn to my mum never to do it again, expecting them to say that I was just scared, and they actually looked relieved, like they didn't have to do it anymore either.

Cold Christmas Church was left in peace for a while but as the next Halloween night approached, Trotsky, the brain of our group had one of his ideas, so like moths to a flame we returned, only this time it wasn't to 'walk the boards'. Trotsky had really excelled himself.

A few months had passed since we had been inside the old church and once again, in a futile attempt to keep us out, the council had tried to secure the tower by boarding the lower windows up. A couple of swift kicks and the new boards lay smashed to bits on the floor above the crypt, leaving the windows gaping, inviting us in.

Kev and Sid lifted me and Trotsky up onto their shoulders, we scrambled in through the yawning window. A bag of straw, which we had collected from a nearby field and five dustbin bags soon joined us, flying in through the window, disappearing into the musty gloom. Once we had located the dustbin bags, we set about filling them up with the straw. As soon as that was completed, we tied the bags together with some string that I had half-inched from the old man, and there in front of us lay a Guy Fawkes dummy. I took Guy for his first and last walk on planet earth, to the spiral staircase and up into the belfry where I pulled a long piece of rope from my pocket, which again my old man had kindly if unknowingly contributed. I wound the rope around Guy's neck, securing it tightly, and hurled him out into the darkness of the tower, where he began to swing in and out of one of the biblical spotlights; now you see him, now you don't, now you see him, now you don't. Trotsky, Sid and Kev were all cracking up laughing down below, hardly being able to control me excitement, I quickly made my way back down the spiral staircase to check out our handy work from the ground up.

Trotsky and me stood back, like two artists viewing their latest masterpiece. Guy switched off and on in the beams of light. Guy looked ghostly, Guy looked terrifying, Guy looked absolutely bloody perfect, the general consensus being that anyone who came up to the old church on Halloween night or any other night for that matter and looked into the church would see a hanged man swinging and, quite rightly, they would shit themselves.

One drawback with Trotsky's idea, was that it was impossible to know who saw Guy and what their reaction might have been, so a couple of days after Halloween we went back to check on Guy, only to find that the council had been back again and not only had they boarded the tower up, but Guy wasn't in residence anymore, there was no sign of him.

Sid kicked one of the new boards off the side of the tower in frustration, which just about summed up the feelings of our group, it had been a lot of work, for little returns, and we had trudged back to the village downcast and forgot all about our swinging Guy.

A few weeks later, I was having tea with mum and the old man.

"Oh, those bloody yobbos!" My mum exclaimed.

The old man tutted, "What is it this time?"

Mum pointed an accusing finger to a feature in the local parish newspaper, she read, "CHURCH HIT BY VANDALS, AGAIN. A group of young brass rubbers from St Mary's Junior School in Ware were spared a fright when visiting St Mary and All Hallows Church, commonly known as the old church in Thundridge, after an eagle-eyed teacher spotted, that louts had broken in and left an effigy of a hanged man swinging in the main tower…"

I suddenly felt frightened, excited, exhilarated, the need to burst out laughing, most of all though, the need to tell everyone.

I chomped my tea down and ran up to Mark's house, told him, we ran onto Kev's, told him and then onto Sid's told him, and finally, Trotsky's. Once we were all together, we hid out in the pit around the back of my house, talking and laughing about it for the rest of the night.

Mark, Sid, Kev and me quite literally rolled around on the floor laughing, calling each other louts, making up our version of the events on that fateful day, the day that the eagle-eyed teacher had saved the children from our swinging Guy, and probably the most funny of them all, Trotsky's assertion that brass rubbers were either metal condoms, robots who wanked regularly, or young men who liked older women.

I didn't know, and I didn't really care what a brass rubber was, one thing I did know, was that I had never seen my mates laugh that much and during that hilarious night, I actually felt that my sides were going to split open, I was laughing so much.

*

I met up with Craig Ruddock, Danny, Phil Buttercroft and Lee and Glyn, outside the village shop at around six o'clock. It was still light, so we waited, sat about talking, smoking a couple of ciggies, until the night had settled in around us properly. In total darkness, we set off up Old Church Lane, out into the open fields, leaving the dwindling lights of the village behind. A couple of stars tentatively revealed themselves high up above in the dark, clouded sky as we left the tarmac of the road, marching onto the gravel track, which led up the old church.

In the distance, we saw the glint of a fire, near the tower.

Craig rubbed his hands together, laughing sinisterly, "It's Halloween time."

The rest of us looked at each other, grinning at the prospect.

"Come on then," Craig egged us on.

Craig, Phil, Danny, Lee, Glyn and me carried on crunching along the gravel track, steadily moving closer and closer towards our intended prey. I could see a roaring fire over the crypt at the front of the church, small figures presented themselves to me and disappeared at once like they were switched off as they walked in between us and the fire. I moved off the crunching gravel track, onto the grass verge to keep the noise down, everyone fell into line behind me, silence crowded in around us.

A gentle breeze like a brush from a long dead spirit stroked my face. I stopped, looking up towards the Thunder ridge, and saw the lights of Cold Christmas glistening in the distance.

Danny walked blindly into the back of me.

I shunted forwards, "Jesus Christ Danny, watch it man, I almost shit my pants."

"Shhh…" Craig warned. "We're too close, they'll hear us!" Snorting to himself.

Cold Christmas Church, the burial ground for a hundred children, loomed up in front of us in all its unflattering glory, strobing eerily in the fire light.

Danny and me ducked down onto our haunches, moving in on the unsuspecting fire starters, to the low outer wall of the graveyard, with as much stealth as we could muster in the hilarity of the situation. It was the perfect vantage point, we peeped over the top.

I saw the roaring fire emanating a blood-red light, that illuminated the side of the church tower and the cypress trees that surrounded it. In and around the flames of the fire, there were maybe five or six kids talking, passing cans around, totally oblivious to our presence. I smiled into Danny's grinning face and reached down, fumbling in the dark, finding a good-sized stone and checked the weight, it was just right.

"I'm a veteran of many a stoning at the all-night garage, watch and learn young Jedi," I said, launching it.

It flew over the top of fire, disappearing into some bushes near the bell tower.

"What was that!?"

One of the fire starters got up, head swivelling, nervously left the right.

"I heard something, there in the trees"

"Oh, shut up, it's just a bird"

"A bird at night?"

"Could be an owl?"

"Oh yeah sure it is, who is it Professor Yaffle, off Bagpuss? We need to get out of here now."

"Professor Yaffle was a woodpecker, you dozy twat."

"I don't care what he fucking was, we need to go, there's so many stories about this place, some of them must be true."

Phil appeared next to me, eyes shining in the murk. "It's Jimmy Beck and his mates, let's leave it, he's alright." He whispered.

"Nah," I said. "This is too good to miss!"

I chucked another one, it ricocheted off the bell-tower, hit one of the surrounding cypress trees, sending a roosting pigeon, crashing through the branches, and it flew off blindly into the night.

"What the fucking hells going on?" Echoed around the graveyard.

"Whatever it is, I don't like it." Came in response.

"I fucking told you, it's not an owl."

"I agree, that was a pigeon."

I had enjoyed this moment a dozen times before; the fear, the confusion, the not wanting, wanting it to be a ghostly apparition, the panic was clearly rising in the group, and we were enjoying every moment of it, it wasn't over yet either it was time to ramp it up another notch.

"Check this out," said Danny.

Danny pulled out his snotty glue sniffers handkerchief from his back pocket, tied it around a huge flint stone, lit it up and chucked it for all he was worth.

Danny's handkerchief Sputnik flew, sparking embers from its tail like Halley's comet, right into the tower, slashing sparks of red, orange, yellow in all directions, the fire starters hit the deck.

"I told you it's not an owl, owls don't spit fire when they fly, it's one of those dead kids, let's get out of here."

"Oh, fuck off, something's not right, it's not dead kids either."

One of them tentatively got up and began to move in our direction, the shadows of the others floating close behind him.

Danny and me were in tears laughing, watching the dying embers of his first moon launch crackling spookily near the tower. I heard the leader of the group's stuttering breath above us as he craned his neck, peeking over the wall.

"AAAAAAAAAHHHHHHHH!" I shouted, bouncing up like a jack-in-the-box.

A whole galaxy of explosions went off behind my eyes as he rammed his head forward onto my forehead, momentary stunning me. I rocked backwards, throwing an optimistic punch in his direction connecting with his cheek, he made a muffled 'Ooof' sound before vanishing back into the gloom of the graveyard.

I shouted, "Oi! OI... Come back... Bastard!" Still dazed.

"Jimmy, Jimmy. It's me, it's Phil, it's me!" Shouted Phil frantically, trying to defuse the situation.

Craig appeared next to me, "What happened Skinner?"

"Someone...Hit me..." I said, still feeling groggy.

"Who did?" Craig insisted.

Danny pointed at the fire starters who were now in a tight huddle around their fire, arms waving, gesturing frantically.

I shouted, "One of those FUCKING BASTARDS hit me!" Pointing along with Danny.

Craig smirked, "Well, what are you going to do about it then?" Challengingly.

I rubbed my aching forehead.

"I WANT TO KNOW WHO DID IT!" I shouted in the fire starter's direction.

"I know Jimmy, it's OK Skinner, I'll go and see what's going on, just stay cool alright?" Phil suggested, still trying to calm things down

Phil re-emerged from the graveyard with a big, long-haired kid, who stood chest out, steadily looking me up and down,

"Yeah, it was me," said, the kid evenly.

"I'll see you outside Beck's house in fifteen," I demanded, "You fucking wanker!"

He nodded, emotionlessly.

Craig reckoned we should let them go back to the village before us, so we stood back, eyeing the fire starters as they trooped past, heads down, they were soon out of sight, so we set off back down Old Church Lane towards the village and Jimmy Beck's.

Craig marched next to me like a duelling second, chanting…

"Come on, Skinner…"
"Come on, Skinner…"

Danny joined in, then Lee and Glyn. Phil silent, the back marker.

"Come on, Skinner…"
"Come on, Skinner…"

I plastered a confident look onto my face, pumping my arm along, inside I was in turmoil.

"Come on, Skinner…"
"Come on, Skinner…"

On one side, I knew I wasn't a good fighter, I was alright when I was at the Junior Mental Institution, had a few fights, got a reputation, having an older brother with a reputation helped too, that is until my older brother's life spiralled out of control, and he started taking his problems out on me, pummelling me regularly. I soon learnt to fear what someone could do to me, rather than what I could do to them; fatal for anyone who is fighting, in fact fatal for any competitor. On the other side, I was angry at being headbutted. I couldn't let that go; there was not only a bit of pride at stake, if I bottled it, that would be my reputation from then onwards; a bottler, and that in turn would lead to more fights.

A vivid imagination wasn't helping either, at the low wall, the kid had looked about five-foot-ten to me, then when Phil had brought him over, he had looked about six-feet, as they did their walk past, he looked about seven-foot-two. I was well nervous, worse still, as my anger abated, my need for retribution dwindled along with it. In a matter of minutes, my confidence ebbed away, looking for a nice quiet corner to hide in; for everyone else though, it was Mardi Gras, the carnival continued.

"Come on, Skinner…"
"Come on, Skinner…"
"Come on, Skinner…"

My second and me walked out of the pitch black of Old Church Lane into the usually welcoming lights of the village, straight ahead underneath one of the lights, basking in its white milky glow, sat Jimmy Beck and his mates. A couple sparked fags on our arrival, then one of stood up, stamping his spent fag under his foot, slouched over in our direction.

Craig nodded to me, "Go on then," he said laying down on his side, propping himself up on his elbow making himself comfortable.

"Come on, Skinner…"
"Come on, Skinner…"

OK come on Skinner, I thought, and marched up to him pushing my arms out, trying to make myself look bigger.

"You're Skinner, aren't you?"

"Yeah, so what?" I said.

"I'm sorry mate. Listen, I don't want any trouble. I didn't know who you were."

I felt stunned, like he had hit me all over again and not just a little bit relieved too, he looked about eight-foot-four now.

I nodded my head, curling my lip up like I was still considering punching him.

"I'm sorry, it was dark up there, I was scared, you jumped out, I didn't know what else to do."

I understood completely, I would have had done the same thing myself, in fact, even Gandhi would have put the head in but Craig and my mates, Jimmy and his mates were all watching.

I, half nodded, begrudgingly, accepting his apology,

"OK, alright, but you'd better fucking watch it, in future," I said, for show.

Nodding back, he turned, walked away, pulling another fag from his pack.

I shrugged my shoulders to my mates, *'what can I do?'*

Jimmy Beck and his mates got up to meet their mate, patting him on the back, then disappeared into his house, leaving the six of us on our own.

Craig made a farting noise like I had bottled out, making Lee and Glyn crack up laughing, "You should have hit him, you let him get away with it, that's sad, Skinner, really sad."

"Oh what, he said sorry, Craig, what was I supposed to do?" I asked.

Craig snorted, "I would have hit him."

"Oh, fuck off, Craig, I don't care what you think." My anger returning.

Craig scowled, dossing me out for a long while, then shook his head aggressively, like he was trying to rid his brain of whatever it was telling him he must do.

"Come on Skinner! Huh… You came on alright Skinner, came on like a girl on her period, what a waste of time, I'm off," he spat over his shoulder.

Craig pounded off towards the bridge, Lee and Glyn close behind.

"Yeah, yeah, yeah… I don't have to do what you want Craig, keep in touch won't you mate," I shouted to his retreating frame.

Chapter Fourteen

Ain't No Feeble Bastard

A few days after Halloween, some of my older punk mates, Trotsky, his brother Ed Fitzwalter, Danny's older brother Pete O'Shea and me decided to have our own fire in the wood that sits next to the disused gravel pit, at the back of Pole's Convent Girl's School. I hadn't seen them for a while as they were all quite a few years older than me, two had moved out of the village, one of them had even got married. It was great to meet up with them again, particularly Pete, as he had been like an older brother to me back in 1977 when my older brother had turned me into his own personal punch bag. Pete had formed a gang and let me join, our name was the S.P.E.N.D. mob, (Skinner, Pete, Ed, Nick and Dave), our soundtrack the Sex Pistols and The Clash, as the five of us chased, chatted up and went out with the posh girls from the convent school.

A huge fire blazed in the middle of us, throwing out welcoming heat, keeping us warm, a couple of carry-outs passing between us as we reminisced about the old days.

"You remember that German exchange student, Olaf, wasn't it?" Pete said.

I laughed, remembering him all too well, "Yeah, I do, you shat in his sleeping bag!"

A crescendo of laughter echoed out across the empty gravel pit.

Trotsky asked, "What!? You shat in Olaf's sleeping bag!?" Raising his voice over the mirth.

"Yeah, he did, I was there, go on tell him Pete, it's hilarious," I replied.

Pete smiled indulgently, "OK Skinner, OK… Once upon a time, there was a twat called Olaf…"

I creased up laughing.

Pete smiled broadly, "No… Nick was doing German A level in the sixth form at school, and he got roped into having a foreign exchange student, Olaf, and he brought all this camping gear along with him; tents, sleeping bags, the lot. We got him to set it up over there," said Pete, pointing towards a flattened down area near the edge of the gaping pit.

"It was perfect, somewhere to bring the convent girls, you remember that Skinner?"

I nodded, "I do mate, Kathy Maher, fucking hell, she was lovely."

Pete grinned knowingly, "Olaf would sleep here in his tent at night and then, because he couldn't be arsed to walk back to Nick's in Ware, he would stay at mine, he was alright to start with, and then he started taking the piss, ordering everyone around."

Ed took a swig from the carry-out, wiping a foamy moustache off his top lip and declared, "I remember him saying 'I'm staying at yours now', like you had no say in it."

"Yeah, that's it, I remember I saw him say 'you will give me my dinner now' to your mum," Trotsky said, laughing at the arrogance of the bloke.

Ed snorted, "You remember when he called home, he was in the phone box, arguing with his mum and dad… He sounded like just like Adolf Hitler."

"I was there. Pete was standing outside with his finger on his top lip, banging his fist down on an imaginary lectern," I said, dissolving into laughter.

Pete cracked up and resumed his tale, "He was a total fucking gobshite, my old dear… Fucking hell, she kept saying to me 'when is he going, when is he going?', he was driving her mad. You know what, the cheeky bastard demanded that she should do his weekly clothes wash. And she did it… I'd had enough."

A smile played at the corner of his lips, while he waited, letting it all sink in, "I told Skinner to wait outside the pub while me, Olaf and Nick had a couple of pints, then as soon as I could get away, I met you outside and told you what I was going to do," he said nodding in my direction.

I cackled, thinking of what was to come, "I didn't believe you, Pete!"

"No, you didn't, did you? You only followed me into the fucking tent. I unzipped his sleeping bag, undid my kecks, squatted down and there you were stood, fucking gawping at me, so I told you to 'fuck off, I can't shit with an audience'."

I nodded at the memory, my face creasing with laughter.

Pete took a last swig from his cardboard carry out, chucked it into the roaring fire, where it crumpled, twisted and melted as the flames took hold.

Pete stretched like he had all the time in the world, which in his case he usually did.

"OK you've built up enough tension now Pete," said Ed, sarcastically.

"I must've had some tension in my bowel that night too, Ed, my arse literally spat out four or five sloppy logs into his sleeping bag. It fucking stank, I can tell you, so I zipped the bag up quickly, gave it a good shake, getting it distributed and engrained."

Raucous laughter echoed off over the dark quarry.

"A few hours later we came back, me and Skinner got into our tent and Nick and Olaf got into theirs next to us, and we waited…"

Pete snorted, suppressing the huge laugh that was forcing its way up from inside him, "I heard them moving about, trying to get comfortable and then, there was an urgent ruffling sound and Olaf said, 'what is vis?' then more ruffling as he basted himself in my shit. And then, 'Nick, Nick, there is shit in my sleeping bag'."

Pete exploded into laughter.

"I tell you me and Skinner were laughing so much it hurt, and then Nick who was pissed out of his head said, 'what are you talking about, you're drunk, go to sleep,' Olaf was shouting, 'no, no, Nick, Nick there is shit in my sleeping bag, look, look' and then for some reason he shouts it out in German too, 'da ist scheisse in mein schlafsack'."

A huge wave of laughter bounced around the open gravel pit.

Pete reflected, "I don't think I saw him again after that or Nick for that matter."

"It's not really surprising though, is it?" Said Trotsky, witheringly.

I sat back and gazed into the fire, watching the shimmering yellows and reds turning into greys and whites, as the flames consumed all in its path, crackling, hissing, sputtering.

A whoosh of sparks flew up onto Ed as something hit the fire.

"OI, THIS IS PRIVATE PROPERTY!" A voice shouted from the dark surrounding woods.

Craig, Sean 'Mac' McDonall and Neil 'Simmy' Simms emerged out of the shadows of the surrounding woods with big grins painted onto their faces.

"What are you lot up to, you boy scouts or something?" Asked Craig, staring down at Ed as he huffily brushed hot ash from his bomber jacket.

Ed opened his mouth to complain, then thought better of it.

Craig saw it all of the time, he would do something totally out of order, then because of his and his ex-boxer brothers' reputations, particularly his oldest brother Don, a county champion who liked to take the boxing ring to the local pubs and discos, he would get away with it. I never doubted their reputation or fighting skills as I had seen and felt it myself over the years, even their old man Don Senior, also an ex-boxer in his mid-fifties, liked to get one in, giving random strangers a dry slap when the fancy took him.

Pete wasn't worried though, "NO! We're having a few brews, what Spaz threw that then?"

"I don't know, maybe it was a squirrel," Craig smirked.

Pete snorted, "Course it was, Craig."

Simmy and Mac laughed sycophantically.

Craig looked around at the two stooges and shook his head, Craig knew what they were doing, he wasn't stupid. Craig's eyes slowly examined the group around the fire, then like a losers' roulette wheel, they stopped on me.

"What arrre you wearing Skinner?"

"It's a destroy shirt," I said, sitting up straight, showing it off proudly.

Craig grinned at the stooges, "Huh, destroy shirt? What do you look like? It looks like a fucking straight jacket!"

"Yeah, it's supposed to, it's a punk t-shirt, The Sex Pistols wore them, you remember them?"

"The Sex Pistols, oh yeah, I remember, they were a bunch of wankers."

Simmy and Mac creased up, agreeing in unison, "Yeah, wankers."

Craig smirked, "Yeah, they, were, wankerssss, Skinner!" Giving me the wankers sign, so there was no doubt about it.

"Fuck off Rubberdick!" I told him, holding his stare.

A loud crack from the fire broke the silence, everyone quiet, watching in anticipation. Nobody called the Ruddock's Rubberdick, not to their faces anyway.

"Yeah?" Craig stood up, shifting himself in front of the fire.

I stood up, Craig's silhouette loomed over me, flame burning at his edges.

BAAAAAMMMM!!!!

A bolt of lightning ripped through my head, I staggered backwards trying to balance, Craig thrust forwards, barging into me, pushing my head up and the starlit sky span backwards above me, his forward momentum taking us over the edge of the quarry, and we rolled down the steep bank into the darkness.

Craig peppered me with vicious body shots to the chest, ribs and stomach, my arms useless, flailing, trying to find some kind of purchase, in the roll.

I'm dead, I'm fucking dead I thought, then I felt something, something I had never felt before; my survival instinct must have kicked in.

I pulled him into me, closing off his body shots, chucking a leg out to stop us rolling, then used everything I had to push myself up and on top of him.

I thought who's the wanker now, laying into him, swinging wildly, punching at his face. Underneath me, he was bucking as hard as he could to get me off, but I wasn't going anywhere.
Craig stopped his futile attempts to get me off and put his elbows up, crossing his forearms over his face to block my punches.

"OK! OK! Skinner Alright, Alright!" He half laughed.

I couldn't have stopped even if I'd wanted too, I wasn't going to stop just because he thought it was over, I was out of control, my mind full of rage, telling me to keep going, going, my body full of pain, driving me on too, all I could see was red, red twisted anger.

"OK, OK, stop Skinner! Stop!" He cried.

Craig's block was solid, so unable to get any punches through, I wedged my hands underneath the protection of his arms, found his neck, and started squeezing, squeezing the fucking life out of him, I gave it everything I had, his now shaking hands tore back at mine trying to release my vice-like grip. All to no avail.

"Pete, Pete! GET HIM OFF! GET HIM OFF! Get him OFFFFF..." He screamed.

I heard a rush of feet, felt hands on my shoulders, pulling at me, shoving me backwards, trying to get me off, I realised what I was doing, oh fucking hell what was I doing? I released my grip, letting the pacifying hands drag me off.

"He's a mad bastard! He tried to strangle me, HE TRIED TO FUCKING STRANGLE ME!" Craig shouted across the open gravel pit.

It's over, I thought. One last downward stare at Craig's sprawling frame, I turned and staggered up the bank with Pete following close behind, he said something… I didn't hear it; I was stunned, didn't know where I was. Pete patted me on the shoulder and I flinched at his touch.

"Are you alright, Skinner?" He asked.

I managed a nod and sat down next to the roaring fire, panting, trying to get my breath back, finally losing myself in the dancing embers, I felt numb, spent, dead inside.

Now and again, Pete would ask me if I was OK, I would nod my head slowly, keeping my eyes focused on the enchanting flames.

A while later, I'm not sure how long, Simmy and Mac hauled Craig out of the gravel pit and sat him in front of the fire, where he too focused on the undulating flames. Craig looked different, younger, vulnerable, broken, I had never seen a Ruddock like that before, nor had anyone else.

"You didn't beat him, Skinner, you're a dirty fighter, you got lucky, he could have you easy!" Simmy said going straight on the attack.

"Oh what? Leave it out Simmy, come on mate!!"

"You shouldn't have done that Skinner, you cheated, he could do you anytime."

I snorted, "OK, I'll see him under the street lights, let's go now!" Firing up again.

Simmy, shook his head, "You should do it here."

I looked at Craig; head down, he was miles away, he wasn't interested.

"OK, come then, let's go over to the street lights, then you won't be able to blind side me again, you bastard."

Craig didn't even look up, just gazed into the fire, lost in the glowing embers.

"I'll fight him in the light, let's go over to the street lights," I said, reiterating my position.

"Ha, you're bottling it," accused Simmy.

"Oh, shut up Simmy, why don't you keep out of it, stop licking his arse, just because you're shit scared of the Rubberdicks," I returned, ready to go at anyone now.

"You want to watch it, Skinner, or I'll give you some," Simmy bristled back.

Pete had had enough, so he stepped in, "Leave it out, Simmy! He's a lot younger than you, he's right, you should keep out of it, they've had a fight, and it's done, let's just leave it, come on let's be honest, Craig doesn't look too interested now does he now?"

"I'm not stopping around here with that cheating little wanker, I'm going," Simmy spat, standing up.

Pete stood up, staring him out, eventually Simmy looked away, knowing he was out of his depth, messing with Pete.

"Come on, let's go, you two coming?" Simmy said to Craig and Mac.

Craig nodded slowly in Simmy's direction, got up shakily, and the three of them disappeared into the darkness of the surrounding woods.

Pete said playfully, "You haven't changed a bit Skinner, have you? You're still a fucking mad bastard," chuckling to himself.

"Jesus Christ Skinner, you ran over him like a T34 tank at the battle of Kursk, nice one comrade," Trotsky said laughing.

Ed thumbed a penny sized hole in his bomber jacket, nodding at his brother's deft analogy, "Nice one Skinner, that'll take the wind out of his sails"

"The Sex Pistols were wankersssss, Skinner," said Pete, mimicking Craig.

A chorus of laughter echoed out across the gravel pit.

*

I was sitting in the lounge watching TV with the old man, the next evening, when Dave came around for me with an anxious expression smeared across his face.

"Craig's waiting down the road for you Skin."

A whole swarm of butterflies took flight in my stomach, I thought oh shit I can't do that again, can I? Can I...? I've got no choice.

"OK, Dave, cheers mate, tell him I'll be there in a minute," I said as casually as I could, reaching for my D.M.s.

Dave gave me a solid nod, pulled a smile onto his face, turned and went to tell Craig.

On went the D.M.'s, I said a polite, slightly desperate goodbye to the old man, like I might never see him again. He nodded, keeping his eyes fixed on the cathode ray tube, spilling out bilge in front of him. I nodded and headed out of the door for round two of a bout, that I didn't want.
Dave stood just outside my front garden, he nodded down the road to Craig, who was sitting on the bonnet of one of
my neighbour's cars, arms folded, waiting calmly. I started walking.

It was a beautiful evening, a low sun rampaged through the cypress trees at the back of the vicarage, throwing bolts of light onto the pavement between us. I strutted towards him, as I got closer, he unfolded his arms, slid down off the car, and we squared up.

"It's light now," Craig said, gesturing with his arms.

I looked around, "Yeah, it is."

An embryo of a smile played at his lips, "What do you want to do then?"

I thought about it for a moment, "Well, what do you want to do?"

Craig pulled an amused face, "You're a mad bastard you are, Skinner."

"I have my moments mate, we all do!"

Craig cracked up laughing, the tension gone, then both of us were laughing.

Dave saw us laughing, saw it was going to be OK, so he wandered down to join us and then the three of us began to discuss the insane night fight in the gravel pit.

A whole hour went by, as we went through every detail. I thought it was strange the way he was laughing about it, I had won, and I didn't think it was that funny, then it dawned on me, maybe it was the boxer's mentality, for him, it was just another fight; yeah, he had lost this one, but he would be ready to fight again, another day - hopefully not with me though.

Craig and me shook hands, burying the hatchet. Before he walked away, he mentioned that his older brother Don was after me for trying to strangle him, but he said he'd have a word with him, which was much appreciated, as I had already had a couple of slaps off Don over the years and I knew nothing in the world would stop him, not even a T34.

Chapter Fifteen

Mr. January in Beastiality Monthly

I still saw Richard around school, but we didn't click like we used to when he was in the band, he seemed different, guarded, even studious, certainly not the same bloke that I used to know. It was like he was reinventing himself, moving on, which was hard to take, after our years of going to gigs together, double-dating the girls, laughing like maniacs and enjoying the chaos of punk rock. If I needed any proof that Richard was changing, buckling down, hitting the books, all I had to do was look at some of the new people he was hanging out with. One of them was Alistair Campbell. I couldn't believe it when I saw him hanging out with the Camp Bell End. I had been walking down the corridor to my next lesson, seen them approaching and Richard looked at me like I had caught him doing something wrong. It was up to him who he hung out with, and now it was up to me to find some new mates, kids who still wanted to fight back; I didn't have very far to look.

Jim 'Cowfucker' Howe and Matt 'Mop Top' Wade were in my form group, we had known each other since the first year and just like me, they hated school and were always up for a laugh, what I didn't know was, they were into punk rock.

Jim, Matt and me were talking, having a laugh, trying to liven up another tedious day at Richard Hole, when I mentioned that I had seen Discharge at the Lyceum over the weekend.

"Oh yeah, did they do Realities of War?" Jim said coolly.

I was a bit taken aback.

"I didn't know you were into them?"

Jim smiled, replying patiently, "I've been into them since that first demo went around, Skinner."

I thought what first demo tape?

"And there was me thinking you were up at your old man's dairy farm fucking cows and all the time you were listening to Discharge," I joked.

"It's all discharge though isn't it," said Matt, evenly.

Jim laughed, "I've been doing both as it goes, haven't you heard of multitasking?"

I smiled, running my hand through my freshly spiked up hair, "Oh what!! Who else do you like then?"

Jim listed out all my favourite bands, and a few I hadn't even heard of.

"You didn't say The Clash, why do you always forget The Clash?" Matt admonished him.

"Err… I don't know, maybe it's because they are shit, you mop head," Jim said.

Matt snorted, "The Clash's first album is one of the best punk albums ever."

"Yeah... It was good, but what happened to them after that?" Jim argued.

"It doesn't matter what happened to them after that."

"Of course, it does, one album doth not a punk band maketh"

"That sounds like Shakespeare," I said interrupting the rapidly escalating debate.

Jim smirked, "I hope not."

"When he leaves this shit hole of a school, he wants to be an actor," he said, pointing at Matt, cracking up laughing.

"Oh well, I'd rather be acting than shafting cows," Matt replied,

"I wouldn't," said Jim, shaking his head dismissively, laughing.

Matt turned to me, a massive smile building up on his face, "Skinner, did you know that Jim here, was Mr. January in the farmer's bi – monthly magazine, 'Bestiality Monthly'?"

"I was Mr. December actually, you mop head," said Jim, trumping him beautifully.

I creased up; immediately I began to feel right at home.

A bright mid-morning sun streamed in through the form room windows, revealing a million particles of chalk dust floating in its searching beams. Jim suggested as it was sunny, we should take a stroll up to The Top Field to see his close mate, Sam Wheatly, who he had seen earlier with a full packet of twenty B&H's.

"OK Jim, nice one, I like a bit of gold service," I said.

Matt nodded his long black curly locks, and the three of us strolled out of the form room.

Richard Hale School had been built on a hill, with an extensive driveway to the front at the bottom, the main buildings in the middle, while the top field sat on the crest of the hill.

In the spring, as the shrubs, small trees and various hedges that marked the edge of the playing field came into leaf, it provided an impenetrable green screen, so whatever we did, fighting, smoking, gambling, letting off fireworks, you could not be seen from the main buildings below.

On the way up, Jim, Matt and me took in some of Richard Hole's most infamous sites. The Gob Pit; a sunken path, that cut between the art block and the outdoor swimming pool, where we would stand on an overlooking wall, gobbing on unsuspecting kids. The shower block where 'wanker' Watson our ex-caretaker had been caught spying on a group of first years sudding themselves in the showers and finally the pièce de résistance. The shallow steps that led up to the top field, where James McCarthy had shit himself on a cross country run. I had seen it with my own eyes; it had been a testing race; the finishing line was close. I was directly behind him, when he had pulled up, arching his back as the cramps took hold, and filled up his pearly white Richard Hale issue shorts with brown rusty water.

Jim, Matt and me sauntered up onto the top field, immediately relaxing, content in the knowledge that no nosy teachers could see what we were up to.

Iain Lancer and Dave Liddell were in conversation, shading themselves under a tree, near the rich green line of vegetation.

"Hey, you boys, put those cigarettes out, won't you?" I Roger 'Lovely Boy, Boy Hopper' Hopkins-ed at them.

I heard raucous laughter and they beckoned us over.

"Richard's been looking for you, Skinner," Iain said.

"Oh yeah, what about?"

"I don't know, something about the band. I think he's playing football in the tennis courts."

I turned to Jim and Matt, who were squinting across the field at a group of kids in a huddle, a haze of white B&H smoke billowing around them.

Jim moaned, "Why is he all the way over there?"

Matt grinned, at us all, "I thought you'd be used to walking in fields."

Jim missed the insinuation, moaned some more, "Oh, fucking hell, we've got to walk all the way over there?"

"It's fine, just pretend this is a cow field and Sam's a big sexy heifer," said Matt, trying to make the walk more enticing for his mate.

I cracked up laughing, "Sorry lads, I better see what that's all about, I'll be back in a minute, save us a Bennie."

Jim eyed Matt, and they plodded off in the direction of the clouds.

I walked back down the shallow steps, around the outdoor swimming pool, past the gob pit and onto the main walkway, which led to the school's side entrance. Once I was passed the side entrance, the whole Lee valley opened up in front of me. All Saint's Church, Hertford, whose ominous bells counted out nine every morning, letting me know I was going to be late for assembly, stood on the right. On the left, the benefits' office, which always made me laugh, it being so close to the school; oh, the irony of it. In the middle, sat between the houses of God and mass unemployment, lay the tennis courts.

I picked out Richard's blonde, grown out skinhead in amongst the mass of white shirts, ducking and feinting as he played football, and headed down.

A huge ball of fire shone down from the clear blue skies above, cooking the tarmac, making the figures of the kids at the far side of the tennis court shimmer, like mirages. I saw blazers stacked high by the wire mesh fence, I saw white shirts open to the waist in a futile attempt to cool down, I saw Camp Bell End, shirt off, tie secured tightly to his head, doing Kung Fu stances, he looked like the Karate kid. 'Wanker on, wanker off', I thought crazily.

"Och aye the noo, Camp Bell, what are you doing?" I said, sarcastically.

Camp Bell End did a quick one-inch punch, fully aware that a group of first years were now watching his deadly moves, "Och ouch den now Baker, I'm a donin me yonder king fu, der new."

I nodded doubtfully.

"Hi Yar!" Camp Bell End announced, kicking out a meandering Bee, missing it by about a foot.

I shook my head, crouching down next to a pillar of blazers watching the game. Richard stormed by, nodded a hello to me, dummied a kid and smoothly passed to Peter Pearman who was sent sprawling to the steaming tarmac by a vicious tackle by Steve Minter.

Richard gave Steve Minter an accusing stare and ran over to Peter to see if he was OK. Peter got up shakily, eyeing Minter as he slotted the ball into the goal at the other end of the court, bringing cheers and baying laughter from his teammates.

I wasn't into football, hadn't played since I'd started wearing bondage trousers, even before that I wasn't very good, but this looked like a laugh, so I asked if I could join in.

A moment later I added my blazer to one of the many teetering pillars, sauntering onto the pitch to play my first game of football in a long time, taking a position on the right wing and received the ball straight away. I passed it to Baldcock who ran in on goal, drawing his foot for a piledriver, only to be clattered to the ground by another industrial challenge from Steve Minter who passed it to Bean, who ran off to score at the other end.

I said, "Oh what, that's a foul isn't it?"

"Bollocks," said Steve Minter, running off to celebrate their goal.

"Fucking cheating wanker," I said, raising my voice at his retreating frame.

Steve Minter stopped and turned on me, scowling, I held his stare.

A couple of his teammates, Jack Frost, and James 'Rusty Waters' McCarthy crowded around him cheering their twenty-sixth goal of the match, he gave me a satisfied smirk, before turning to join in with the celebration, bouncing in the throng.

Peter Pearman dispiritedly took the ball back to the centre circle, for another kick off.

"I wouldn't worry about it Baker, it's always the same when he plays," he said passing the ball to me.

It bounced up off a bump in the tarmac hitting my ankle, running away from me and as I went after it, Steve Minter came ripping right through the back of me, knocking me forward, pushing me down on my haunches, I just about managed to stay on my feet.

A couple of his teammates laughed at my hapless gait, I span around on him, he was off, his eyes fixed on the ball as it bounced off up the court.

I bellowed, "You fucking Wanker."

Steve Minter came straight at me and smacked me hard in the face. I recoiled and threw a couple of punches back, one hitting nothing, the other connecting with his forehead. He shrugged it off like it was nothing, advancing on me with even more fervour, smashing two more into my face, I fell back, trying to avoid the onslaught, he advanced.

I belted him hard in the stomach several times, once again he didn't seem to feel a thing, he just kept coming, chalking up another direct hit on my face.

A right hook to his jaw didn't stop him, he just threw two punches back, so I grabbed his arms, trying to wrestle him to ground, trying to stop his rampaging fists, he was way too strong though, threw me off like it was nothing and as my head came up, he hit me left-right, twice in the face, I staggered backwards, and he moved in to dish out some more punishment.

"OI! WATCH IT, THERE'S A TEACHER COMING!" Richard warned.

Steve Minter and me broke, looking up towards the side entrance and saw Mr. Cyril 'Thunderbirds are Go' Thurl gesticulating frantically, like an imbecile with semaphore flags.
Steve Minter and me just looked back at each other and burst into fits of laughter.

"You're a good fighter," I said, holding out my hand, knowing I'd lost the fight, hoping to win the peace.

Steve Minter shook it firmly and said, "Cheers, are you alright?"

I touched my face, surprisingly, it felt OK, "I'm fine mate," I said, confidently.

"You can half take a punch," Steve Minter grinned.

I thought yeah, and you can't half throw one too. "My old man always said I had a hard head," I replied laughing.

I heard the bell go, signalling the end of break and that the afternoon lessons were about to begin, thankfully ending the game of football before Steve Minter's Gladiator-like challenges could do anymore damage to anyone.

Richard came up to me, fastening his tie, "Jesus, Skin, are you alright?" He asked, with a concerned look on his face.

I sniffed a couple of times, jabbed a finger into my itching nose, picking out a dark bloody bogie, and flicked it in the direction of Karate Kid Camp Bell End, who backed away.

"Yeah, I'm fine mate, this football's a rougher game than I remember."

Richard patted me on the shoulder, smiling at my bravado, "Are sure you're, OK?"

"Richard... I'm, fine, mate," I said, belligerently.

"Don't worry, Rich, he didn't knock my blockhead off."

Richard cracked up laughing, "Come on, we better get going, or we'll be late."

Richard and me walked back up towards the main buildings.

"Cheers for shouting, Rich, I was losing badly there, "I said, scratching at my nose again.

"You were," He said, sniggering.

"I can't believe it. Skinner was saved by a teacher, I never thought I would ever say those words."

"I know mate, my street credibility is in tatters."

"Well, it was Thunderbirds, he did an international rescue on you," Richard quipped.

I creased up as we approached Richard's class.

"OK, I might see you about then Rich?"

"Yeah, yeah, of course Skin, it's been good talking to you again, where are you hanging about now?"

"I'm round the front with Jim and Matt."

"I don't see you enough these days, we need to catch more, I'll tell you what, why don't you come up to The Gob pit tomorrow, I'll tell Stephen and Dave."

"OK mate sounds good," I nodded; it would be good to see Stephen Barnes again too, "How is Stephen these days?"

"Oh, he's OK, I saw him a couple of days ago, he's got a cold, he was saying he'd like to go to The Gob pit, to make the most of it."

I creased up, 'make the most of it', it really would be good to see Stephen Barnes again.

Richard's Maths teacher, Robert 'Robot Ahh B.9.X.' Caxton bustled passed us, his hands full of books, giving us a 'that's the end of your conversation look'.

"OK mate I will, see you."

"See ya then, Skin."

I walked off, slapped my forehead remembering, "Richard what did you want to see me about?"

"Oh crikey, yeah, shit sorry Skinner, Andy's not going to be able to come to band practice Saturday, he's going to a boxing match with the old man."

"Oh what? I almost get my blockhead knocked off, now there's no practice Saturday, what a fucking day."

Richard grimaced playfully, following Robot Ahh B.9.X. into class.

Chapter Sixteen

Nigel Osbourne Gets Launched

Jim, Matt and me headed straight for The Gob Pit, at first break the next day, where we found Stephen Barnes, Dave Liddell, Richard and Frances 'Van Ears' Van Hage in rapt conversation.

Dave looked up and saw Jim approaching, "Mooooooooooooo," he mooed, mournfully.

"Leave it out Dave, he'll get a hard on," I said, grinning.

"Oi, Cuboid and you Flopsy bunny, what are you doing out of your burrow?" Jim said, smirking at us both.

Dave gave him a toothy smile.

Dave Liddell and me had been mates since Richard's face and the platform at Ware station had first connected, we had hung out in Tracks, bunked the Hertford train on numerous occasions, and I had been up to his house in Ware, to listen to his vast record collection. I hadn't spoken to Frances Van Ears before, knew only two things about him; one was what my old man had said about his family business, Van Hage's garden centre; that 'it was a rip off, they sold pebbles for ten pounds each', and two was what everyone else knew about him, he had massive dinner plate sized ears.

I felt a sorry for him, he used to grow his hair long to try to cover them up, he had no chance, they still looked like two observatory satellite dishes protruding from either side of his head, even with long hair. I thought, if he really wanted to cover them up, he would either have to put a big fucking sack over his head or not go out in daylight.

I strolled up and looked to Dave, "Alright, how's your old man these days, Dave?"

Dave gave me a knowing smile, "Oh he's fine Skinner, hasn't heard any bad language lately."

"What's that all about?" Asked Richard.

"It's classic, I was around at Dave's last week, up in his bedroom and he put on that album 'New Boots and Panties'."

I noticed Andrew Thornley ambling along the sunken path towards The Gob Pit, totally oblivious to the danger he was walking into. I nudged Stephen, who in turn nudged Richard, who grinned at me, eyes twinkling in anticipation.

"Yeah, so Ian Dury, it's the album that starts with all that swearing, Dave had just cued it up and his man walks in, and 'Arseholes, bastards, fucking cunts and pricks' comes blaring out of the speakers, his old man goes 'I beg your pardon', laughs and walks out again."

I turned, smirking at the hapless Thornley.

"You alright Andrew?" I said, springing the trap.

Stephen let loose, gobbing a huge influenza-filled, yellow grolly into his hair.

A seven spit salute began.

Pttt, Pttt, Pttt,
Pttt, Pttt Pttt, Ptt.

The air was full of flob.

Andrew Thornley turned to run out of the rain of phlegm. Jim missed completely. Matt just missed. Frances got his own leg. Dave caught him with spray. Richard got him a beauty on his arm, and my late entry into the gob fest got stuck, swinging pendulum-like from his back, as he legged it, glancing back laughing, sticking his fingers up at us.

Clive 'Hair Bear' Harper, my form teacher, appeared from behind the art block, raising his hand to slow the bullet-like Thornley down, then gesturing, he pointed at the flob in his hair. Andrew Thornley was in my form group, he was OK, I doubted he would grass us up but just to be on the safe side, we slipped away, around the side of the swimming pool, and up the shallow steps, sometimes named as McCarthy's steps, to the sanctuary of the top field.

Once we had found a nice, secluded spot, near the rich green tree line at the edge of the rugby/crickets pitch, Frances Van Hage pulled out a brand-new pack of B&H's, casually spilt the plastic with his thumbnail and generously offered them around.

Stephen Barnes announced, "Steve Minter's been suspended." Through a mouthful of smoke.

"What really? Why?" Dave asked.

"Ah, he's been a very naughty boy, you know that nice-looking lab assistant Kerry, the one that works with Butter man Bagley."

Matt nodded, toking on the expensive tobacco, while Jim panted like a dog, showing his appreciation of the lovely Kerry, causing a few sniggers.

"Yeah, that's her Jim, white lab coat, big smile, big knockers, well he only flashed his cock at her didn't he and she said if you do that again, I'll report you and what did he do? He did again, so that was it, he was sent home this morning."

"I doubt he'll be back then," Richard said, flicking ash off his B&H.

"Nah it won't be worth it, there's only a few months to go till we're out of here for good," I said making a fist in triumph, at the thought of no more school.

"Yessss, can't come soon enough," said Matt at the prospect.

Jim shook his head in distaste, confiding, "It doesn't surprise me, Steve Minter was a weirdo, you remember when he put his dick on Michael Day's shoulder in the library?"

"Oh yeah, that was hilarious," said Matt, mouth billowing out smoke.

Jim shook his head grumpily, "No, it wasn't."

"It was when Greg 'The Little Gestapo' Young's wife saw it and started wailing," Matt retorted, his face creasing up with laughter.

"I saw that, it was fucking brilliant, I thought she was going to pass out," I said, cackling manically, remembering the look on the stupid old bag's face.

"Poor old girl, she probably hadn't seen a dick in ages," said Stephen, grinning.

"Greg Young is a dick; she sees him every day," stated Richard, factually.

Dave said, "Oh well that's the end of Steve Minter then, he definitely won't be back," pulling his lips onto his teeth.

Frances smirked at me, "I bet you're pleased he's gone, aren't you Baker?"

"Nah, not really, he's alright... I don't like it when someone flashes their cock at my bird though," I said not rising to it, making everyone crack up.

Richard said, "Your bird? Ha! She's not into cuboids," puffing out a pall of smoke and sang. "Kerry's not feeling alright with the cube." Paraphrasing the 999 song, making everyone crease up again.

I blew out a crest of white smoke, "Oh what, that's a little bit harsh isn't it, Richard?"

"Harsh realities of life, my friend," said Richard, completing the mantra.

"Harsh realities," Jim echoed, chuckling to himself.

I snorted, "It's very harsh actually, maybe she could teach you how to kiss Richard," getting down on my knees, opening my arms wide, beseechingly.

"Oh, please Kerry, teach me how to kiss," I said puckered up, sending everyone into stitches.

Frances said, "Or Dave could mate with her and have lots of little bunny wabbits."

"No, he's a wanking wabbit," Richard corrected.

"Fuck off L plates," said Dave happily.

Stephen, who had seemed distracted held up his hand, "Hold up, hold up watch this."

Nigel Osbourne, a kid I knew from my form group, approached us.

"Is it your birthday today Osbourne?"

"Yes… Er… No!"

Immediately realising his mistake, he legged it as fast as his sturdy legs could carry him. Nigel Osbourne got about twenty-feet before Richard brought him to ground with a perfectly timed rugby tackle, and we all ran over laughing, viewing his catch.

"Buuuuummmpppss!" We all shouted.

Nigel Osborne creased up, "OK, OK, but not too high though, not too high."

I looked to Richard, he looked back at me knowingly, we both grinned.

A big heave and the seven of us hefted Osbourne up, holding him up by his legs and arms.

"Happy birthday to Obo, Happy birthday to Obo, Happy birthday to Obo, Happy birthday to Obo," we sang, all grinning at each other.

Once we had finished serenading Obo with his birthday song, it was now time for the bumps for the birthday boy, we began to lift him up and lower him down again.

"One, two, three, four, five…"

It started off gently.

"Six, seven, eight, nine, ten, eleven twelve…"

Higher and higher…

Once we hit the teens, that was it, a mixture of our adrenaline and who could be the maddest bastard meant we totally lost control and as the number got higher, so did he.

On 'Thirteen' he was a foot above our heads, laughing his head off.

'Fourteen', he was two-foot above our heads, still laughing.

On 'Fifteen' he was flying three-foot above our heads, flapping his hands like a bird, trying to stop himself from flipping over, he wasn't laughing anymore, we were though.

On the sixteenth bump, we caught him, lowering him down, he let out a huge sigh of relief, he had survived, his ordeal was over now. Obo grinned back up at us, but we hadn't quite finished yet; we needed to wish the birthday boy the best of luck, so we started swinging him backwards and forwards, towards the rich green tree line, chanting…

"One for luck,
Two for luck,
Three for the old man's…"

On the word 'coconut', we launched him high into the air…

Nigel Osbourne hurtled into the shrubbery, disappearing beneath the thick canopy, sticks cracking and snapping as he went. A deathly silence followed.

Stephen gaped at me, his mouth, a mirror image of mine, a horrified 'O' shape.

Dave said, "Oh, shit, oh shit, oh shit." Summing up the group's feelings.

"Oh, fucking hell," Jim said, expressing our feelings even better.

Richard laughed nervously.

"Oh no, we've really done it this time," My voice full of regret.

Richard ran down into the bushes, the rest of us close at his heels and there in amongst the shrubbery we saw Nigel Osbourne's limp body splayed out, pathetic, unmoving, emanating a low mewling sounding.

Richard said, "Oh Jesus, are you alight mate?" Placing a reassuring hand on his shoulder.

Nigel Osbourne jumped up laughing, "Oh my word, you should have seen your faces," he said.

I thought oh thank fuck for that. Dave and Richard let out relieved sighs in unison.

"I'm fine, the trees broke my fall," said Nigel suddenly rubbing at his arm, inhaling sharply.

"Ouch, oh no hold on… Oooohhh," he said, with a sudden intake of breath.

"Nigel, are you sure, you're OK?" Asked Richard, his face a picture of concern all over again.

"Oh my, I got you again, didn't I?" he laughed.

"Cheeky little bastard," said Richard, grabbing his arm.

"Let's give him the bumps again."

Jim and Matt moved forwards and he cowered away.

Stephen said, "No, come on, leave it out, he's OK, I would shut up if I was you Obo."

"He's OK, aren't you, mate?" I insisted, patting him on the head firmly.

"Yes, yes, of course, of course," he blustered.

"I have learnt a rather important lesson today, never tell anyone at school that it's your birthday."

Stephen, Richard, Dave, Frances, Jim, Matt and me all cracked up laughing at Obo's logic, said goodbye to the brave and now wiser kid, and walked back up through the rich green tree line to continue with the issues of the day and Frances's packet of B&H's. I thought, yeah, I've been at Richard Hole for almost five years now, and I've never had a birthday.

Chapter Seventeen

End Product

A far off ringing awakened me from my slumber, telling me it was lunch break, so I tossed my Virus V1 logoed maths book into my desk, slamming the lid shut on it, gave Jim a nod and together with Matt we set off for the gob pit.

In the side entrance to the school, a fresh breeze blew in across the playground, greeting our exit, I filled my lungs, exorcising the dust of the stale classrooms of the morning. I looked away beyond the perimeter, it was another fine, too beautiful to be cooped up in the classroom day. A high bank of cirrus stratus clouds scudded easily across a perfect blue sky, soft contrails criss-crossing it left by aeroplanes as they flew off to far away places.

I sighed deeply, trying to take it all in…

I felt cleansed
I felt revitalized
I felt oh… Shit.

Alistair Camp Bell was standing with Stephen, Richard, Dave and Frances at the edge of The Gob Pit, hands gesticulating widely, telling them something they should know.

Jim hesitated, "Oh fucking hell, look who it isn't."

I snorted, "Come on Jim, let's go over, if they think he's alright he can't be that bad, can he?" I said, stretching my arms out, crucifix like.

"Are you asking me?" Said Jim, a grin playing at his lips.

"Come on, if he's being a wanker, we'll go around the front."

"We may as well just go around the front then," said Jim, cracking up.

"Brace yourself, young Jim, we're going in," said Matt, steeling himself.

Jim scratched his big hooter, "Shut up, Biggles."

Matt, Jim and me wandered over to join the group, the moment Camp Bell saw us, he pushed his chest out, and proclaimed, "I'm a member of a gang in Hatfield, we're all black belts in Kung Fu, we're always fighting with the kids from the local council estate," in a loud voice.

Nobody knew what to say, seven amused faces looked off into the distance, trying to hold back the mirth that was welling up inside them.

Jim whistled the Carl Douglas one hit wonder 'Kung Fu fighting', sending everyone into fits of laughter, all apart from the irked Camp Bell who stared at Jim. Who in turn held his stare, waiting for Richard Hole's answer to Bruce Lee to materialise, but nothing happened.

Jim sighed deeply at the lack of Kung Fu fighting, it was neither frightening nor fast as lightening.

"I'm off down the front, you coming?" He said to Matt and me.

I looked to Richard, who was now trying to hold back waves of laughter, hoping to spare his mate any more embarrassment.

"Yeah, definitely, I'll see you fast as lightening cats later," I said, passing my eyes over the still fuming Camp Bell as we walked off.

Once we were out of harm's way, Matt, Jim and me made our way down to our usual haunt, around the front of the main buildings, near the art block, finally coming to rest under the enormous crab apple tree, near the main road. I couldn't work out why they had chosen to hang out down there at first, as it was in full view of the nearby staff room, therefore impossible to have crafty fag, then Matt explained.

"I know there's no smoking but look there's a road and there's a crab apple tree," grinning from ear to ear.

"OK, and?" I enquired, not seeing what he was going on about.

Matt had snatched a handful of rotten crab apples off the ground, lobbed them as hard as he could at a passing white van, then he hit the deck, leaving me standing there like a lemon as the van's brake lights flashed an angry red, and it came to a screeching halt.

Jim grinned up at me with a 'what the fuck are you doing up there?' face, good point I thought and fell to the ground next to him.

A few minutes of laughter and the odd shout of wanker, we heard the van slowly move off.
Matt tentatively popped his head up to see if the coast really was clear, seeing no agitated van drivers about, of which there were none, so we all stood up.

"Crab apple tree. Road. Elementary, my dear Watson," Matt deduced conclusively.

I smiled, nodding thoughtfully, I had just learnt an important lesson.

In the midday heat, it was too much effort to hassle the passing traffic, so we behaved ourselves, lounging under the crab apple tree discussing the merits of Discharge's new single 'Decontrol'.

"I like it, it's a bit repetitive though, not as good as the stuff on 'Why'," I said.

"It's too slow," stated Jim, nodding.

"Too slow!!! No, it's brilliant and their production's getting better," countered Matt.

"It's not about the production, it's about energy," said Jim, warming up.

"Yeah, but it's better to have both, though."

Richard ran up to us, clearly shocked, killing off the embryonic discussion.

"Oh my god, have you heard Stephen Barnes' been expelled," he said out of breath.

"Oh what, nah, surely not?" I said, from the cool shade under the

crab apple tree.

Jim laughed, "That doesn't surprise me, he's a nutter."

"Yeah, he only had a go at Greg 'The Little Gestapo' Young, didn't he?" Richard said, laughing despite himself.

Matt sat up, brushing at some of the scuffs on his black D.M.s, "What happened then?"

Richard took a deep breath, we were all silent, wanting to know what happened to one of, if not the finest of Richard Hole's hooligans.

"OK, OK, right, it's unbelievable. I was standing with him in the dinner queue and the little Gestapo officer walks past us, sees he's not wearing a tie and asks where it is and Stephen says 'I don't need to wear it, I've got asthma, I've got a letter from the doctor' and the Gestapo gets shirty, says, 'well at least tidy up your collar' and goes to put it straight, Stephen says 'oi don't touch me, you're not allowed to touch me', the Gestapo says 'I can, and I will' and then Stephen pushes him away... Fucking woo wobs you should have seen the Gestapo's face, he was furious he says 'I need you to come with me now Barnes' and Stephen says..." Richard creased up laughing, taking a moment, shaking his head in disbelief.

"You won't believe this... He says, 'no not now, I'm busy, I'm about to have my dinner, maybe later'."

People stopped playing football in the tennis courts, looking over at the avalanche of laughter coming from under the crab apple tree. Matt was rolling around on the floor holding his side, all concern about his scuffed-up D.M.'s totally forgotten.

"No, not now, I'm busy, I'm about to have my dinner, maybe later, fucking hell, the bloke's got some front," Jim stated.

It was just as funny the second time, we fell about all over again.

I said, "I knew he was a mad bastard… Fucking hell," through tears of laughter.

"What a hero, someone should write a song about him," said Matt.

Jim nodded, stretched back and sung, "I ain't no feeble bastard, no fucking scapegoat, that's Discharge by the way." Pointedly looking at Richard.

"I know, Andy, my little brother plays them all the time, he loves them," replied Richard confidently.

I said, "I bet you love that," pouring on the scorn, still holding my aching sides.

Richard laughed, "I like the new single 'Decontrol'."

A smiling Jim said, "That's another one for Stephen."

"Oh, come on, Richard you don't like Discharge," I said.

"No, not really, I've been playing some of the old stuff again though."

"Oh yeah, like who?" I said, sceptically.

"The Pack, The Buzzcocks, The Ruts and the Clash, I still like The Clash."

Jim interjected, "The Clash aren't punk."

Matt put his head in his hands, "Oh fucking hell, here we go again"

Richard looked at them both quizzically.

I sighed. I shook my head. I explained. "I wouldn't worry about it Rich; some people wonder why we are here and the futility of life, some wonder if we really exist at all, meanwhile these two are still stuck on whether The Clash is a punk band or not."

"They are!" Claimed Matt.

"Bollocks," counterclaimed Jim.

"You've got shit for brains, Jim; you could grow grass on your head," replied Matt.

I buried my head in my hands, thinking this could go on for a while, "I need a ciggie, I'm off to the top field, anyone up for it?"

"Yeah, OK," Richard said, quickly followed by The Clash-a-phile and the non-believer.

Matt slapped his head, "Oh fuck, I almost forgot," he said, grabbing a handful of crab apples.

"Oh yeah, lemon entry my dear Watson," I replied, picking up a few myself.

"Mind if I join in?" Chimed Jim.

"It wouldn't be the same without you," said Matt.

Once the three of us were armed and not particularly dangerous, we strafed the cars waiting at the traffic lights outside the benefits office and as the crab apples rained down on bonnets, wings and windscreens, we legged it up to the sanctuary of the top field.

On the bus home that evening, in amongst the other drones scratching out a living or serving their time in the none-education system like myself, I started thinking about what Richard had said about listening to punk again. The Pack, The Ruts and The Buzzcocks weren't as heavy as us or any of the emerging Anarchist punk bands that the punks were into now, but the more I thought about it, the more I thought, I should ask him to rejoin the band.

OK, when he left, he had said that he wasn't into punk anymore, from what he said this afternoon, though, he was back into again. If he still wanted to play different types of music that would be fine too, maybe this time around, we could record them, keep them, and work on them as a side project to Virus V1.

I suppose when it really came down to it, the band was missing his sense of humour, particularly his younger brother and although Whiff had turned out to be a decent bass player and was fully committed to the band, once he had settled down, he became more relaxed around us, came out of himself, Dave had found some of the things he was coming out with difficult to digest, and I had already had to have a word with him after one practice.

Richard got on well with Dave, in fact he got on well with everybody, he was my best mate. If that wasn't enough, his own brother was in the band, how could he not want to come back? I made my mind up, the next time I saw him, I was going to ask him, see what he says, what's the worst that could happen? As for Whiff, I would have to cross that bridge when I came to it.

A few days later, Richard and me were on the top field having a crafty fag, while I was telling him that I had been over to Jim's place the night before.

"I saw no evidence of cow fucking whatsoever," I claimed.

Richard laughed, "He must do it at night, he's a secret cowfucker."

I sang, "Jim's trying to get it up, and it's one of those nights. Cow shite. All night," Paraphrasing the R. White's lemonade advert on TV.

"You should do a punk version of that," Richard said, grinning.

I snorted, "It was a weird set up though Rich."

"Explain?"

"When I saw his mum and old man, I thought they were his grandparents, I almost asked where his mum and Dad were."

Richard leaned forwards laughing, "I saw them at Founders Day last year and I thought exactly the same thing."

"Grandad… Grandad… You're lovely…" He sang.

I creased up laughing, joined in, "That's, what, we, all, think, of, you…"

"Poor old boy, making Jim must have almost killed him."

Richard gave it some thought, "What about Grandma, birthing that nose?"

"Oh what, that's a little bit harsh isn't it?"

"Harsh realities of life, my friend," replied Richard.

"Nah Jim's alright, he's a good bloke, you should see him when he comes into a class late, he scowls at the teacher, no matter who it is, slams the classroom door, slams his bag down, slams the desk lid, he's like a grumpy old man sometimes," I said.

Richard smiled, "I've seen it. It's classic, yeah, he's alright."

"And he's into good music," I said, awkwardly moving the conversation on in the right direction.

"Yeah, he does, The Clash are brilliant."

I didn't bother to correct him. I thought it's now or never.

"Rich mate, why don't you come back and join the band?"

Richard looked down, staring into the grass, "Hmm… I don't know, Skin," He said quietly.

"Oh, come on mate, it'll be a great laugh, like the old days."

"No, Skin, sorry I can't," he said running a finger over his teeth.

"Why not?" I asked, insistently.

"I don't want to."

"You can't? You don't want to? I don't get it, why?"

Richard looked up, "BECAUSE... I DON'T WANT TO!" He said, forcefully.

"OK, cheers mate, thanks a lot," I said, sarcastically, surprised by his anger.

Richard spat, "Skinner, look, I got you a new bass player... I'm not coming back... And that's it."

And that really was it, he stormed off.

Oh great, I thought, not only have I lost a decent bass player, but I've lost a good mate too, I trooped off in the opposite direction.

Once I had got over the initial disappointment of him not rejoining the band, I couldn't work out whether I was upset or pissed off. Upset with myself for asking him, or pissed off with him saying no. It went around and around in my head for days; I just couldn't work it out. Pissed off or upset? Upset or pissed off? I had no answer.

In the end, he made it easy for me, when he came to school sporting a new romantic's style wedge haircut. Richard and me hadn't spoken since he had said no to rejoining the band on the top field, and then he randomly came up to me while we were lining up for the final fifth year school photo, like he was making sure that I saw the new romantic's abomination; I hated the new romantics and the yuppy culture that had spawned around it; he knew that.

"You alright, Skinner, can you hold these for me?" He said, holding out some exercise books.

I shrugged my shoulders huffily, "Huh, yeah, OK," I said, taking the books from his outstretched hand.

A couple of minutes later, he came back grinning from under his wedge. "Cheers."

Richard saw I was frowning at his new haircut, "Oh yeah I got a wedge, I guess I'm just a dedicated follower of fashion."

He took back his books and promptly disappeared into the crowd of kids, making themselves ready for their final year photograph.

I thought, what a bell end and yep, I should be upset with myself for asking him, it was stupid, thank fuck I didn't say anything to Whiff.

*

A few months crawled past in the blink of an ice age and as my time at Richard Hale slowly wound down to its end, the O level examinations began. I knew I would fail them all, as I had stopped taking notes in the middle of the fifth year. I had even given up on my two best subjects; History and Economics, after I had achieved decent B grades for them in my mocks.

Mr. 'Morose' Moore and 'Hair Bear' Harper, my economics and history teachers, respectively, had watched my interest in their subjects wilt and die over the last year. 'Morose' and the 'Hair Bear' had done their best to bring me around, mixing praise and punishment, but I just wasn't interested, and soon I became a lost cause to them. Morose found it easier for himself, if he let me sit at the back of his class and do what I wanted to do, as long as I wasn't disturbing anyone, and what I wanted to do, was write lyrics for Virus V1 tracks; music was my life now. The gigs were brilliant. The albums being released were getting heavier and my guitar playing was improving by the day.

In my last Economics' lesson before the exam, I wasn't in the mood for writing lyrics, so I took out a pack of playing cards, challenging myself to build the biggest card castle that had ever been seen in an economics class. It was a tough job, but someone had to do it. I meticulously built the first level doubling the cards up, giving it a stronger foundation and again a second layer of backing cards for the base of the second level. A ruler against the structure told me my handy work was excellent, it was perfectly level, it had passed the test. On the next test, I pushed my forefinger against the construction, finding it to be strong, resisting the pressure I had brought to bear upon it. Once I had made the strong foundations, it was easy, I continued the process until I had topped it with the tricky sixth level, and then happy, I sat back to take in my edifice. Inspecting it, I found it to be, a perfect six across, six up, house of cards.

A couple of kids noticed, nodded their heads in appreciation of my deft handy work, another couple laughed, alerting Morose that something was afoot in his, now not so silent, revision class.

"Oh yes, very good, you can throw your future away if you like Baker, but have a little consideration for your fellow students, put that away."

I smirked at him, shrugged my shoulders, "Why? It's a perfect representation of Maslow's hierarchy of needs, in fact it's even better, it's got an extra layer, Sir."

"OK Baker, you've got what you wanted, get out and stand in the corridor," Morose shouted pointing at the door.

I slouched out of his class, selflessly leaving my monument to society's needs intact, for others to enjoy. Once I was out in the corridor, I thought bollocks to this, I'm not hanging around in here like some knob end, I'm going up the top field for a fag.

I pushed the fire door open and there was Richard stepping towards me, hair neatly combed, top button done up, dressed in a light-brown Macintosh, a briefcase in his hand.

I snorted, he glared back, daring me to say something.

I thought, what happened to you, mate? We were the punks, we were going to change the world, now look at you, you've changed into them and then suddenly, it all became clear. Richard had been going through a phase, now that phase was over, he was moving on, whether he had come to that conclusion by himself or he had been prompted, I didn't know, didn't care either. I wondered when my phase would be over. I ran my hand through my hair making sure it was spiked up properly, thought never, and strutted off across the playground.

A week later I went in for my last exam, geography, it was also my last day at Richard Hole. Whilst I waited outside the examination hall, wasting my time, feeling bored, I eavesdropped on Camp Bell talking to fellow briefcase carrier Roger 'The Todger' Chislett. I couldn't believe exactly what I was hearing, Camp Bell wasn't interested in kung fu fighting the council estate kids as fast as lightening anymore, he had other plans now.

"If I get the right grades here, I will by the way, Roger, I'm going to go to university. If I get the right grades there and I ruddy well will, Roger, I'm going to get a job in my dad's accounting company in London. I'm going to work my blinking socks off, make my pile and retire early at fifty-five years old, I'll be able to do what I want then."

"Yes, sounds fantastic, Alistair," said the Todger, agreeing wholeheartedly.

I thought, fucking hell, why would anyone want to do that? You're going to miss the summer of your life, start living in autumn, then you can do what you want? Do what exactly?

Join the bowls club?
The neighbourhood watch, perhaps?
Knitting maybe?
The local rambling society?
How about being a philatelist?
A course in cake making?
Learn how crochet?
A bit of scrabble, perchance?
Play a bit of golf?
Go fly-fishing with J.R. fucking Hartley?
Or maybe go on a cruise, watch the world drift past your window all over again?

Fuck off, what a waste, it just didn't make any sense, whatever he did, he would never get those precious, precious, years back again. I mean seriously, how could a supposedly intelligent kid like that miss the whole point of what life was – to live.

A couple of hours later, I carefully wrote Bichael Maker into the name box at the top of my geography paper and took a quick look back over my handy work. A feeling of satisfaction passed through me, I hadn't answered a single question, the exam paper was completely blank.
I smiled to myself, stood up, handed my perfect paper into 'Robot Ahh… B.9.X' Caxton, who beeped something unintelligible back in my direction, and I was done.

I sauntered out of the examination hall, down the steps and looked across the grounds, thinking I've been coming here for the last five years, now it's over, I can't think of any reason why I will come back here again, ever; I'll never see this place again, I swear it.

A cobalt sky of opportunity above me, I took my first post Richard Hole breath, it felt good, very good, so I took another one, one of many to come I thought, and walked out of the grounds for the last time, towards the bus station in the middle of Hertford.

Richard Hale School disappeared behind me, as I paced down the steps of the underpass in front of All Saint's Church, looking up, I wondered why the bells weren't ringing out in celebration.

I chuckled to myself, thinking thank fuck that's over, five years of old school tie bullshit; not anymore. I'm in control now. I'm free to do what I want when I want, then charitably, I thought, it hasn't been a complete waste of time coming to Richard Hale School for all these years. I have learnt a lot… Outside of the classroom.

Printed in Great Britain
by Amazon